WRINKLIES™
Wit &
Wisdom

WRINKLIES™
Wit &
Wisdom

Quotations and Observations
for the Chronologically Challenged

Rosemarie Jarski

PRION

First published in Great Britain in 2005.
This edition published in 2017 by Prion
an imprint of the
Carlton Publishing Group
20 Mortimer Street
London W1T 3JW

1 3 5 7 9 10 8 6 4 2

A catalogue record for this book is available from the British Library.

ISBN 978-1-85375-985-7

Printed in Dubai

To Mum,

younger than springtime are you

Contents

Introduction

This collection of wrinklies' wit and wisdom is a book for anyone who's getting older and, last time I checked, that was everyone! The contributors laid bare inside this meaty tome – John Mortimer, The Golden Girls, Barry Cryer, Elaine Stritch and many more – are inspirational role models for any age, young or old, too. They never pass their amuse-by dates; their wisdom is timeless. Most of the contributors can ride the buses for free so they speak with the voice of experience. They shoot from the hip – real or titanium – sharing the pleasures as well as what Byron called 'the woes that wait on age'. Wrapping those woes in wit doesn't make them go away but it does make them a bit more bearable. If laughter is the best medicine, consider this book the perfect prescription for ageing well and living a full and happy life.

So, feel free to pop a few pearls of wit and wisdom every day. For those who do, I guarantee that Her Majesty's telegram celebrating your centenary is practically in the post. After all, he who laughs, lasts.

Enjoy!

Age is Just a Number

I'm very pleased to be here. Let's face it, at my age I'm pleased to be anywhere.

George Burns

He was either a man of about 150 who was rather young for his years, or a man of about 110 who had been aged by trouble.

P.G. Wodehouse

Age is a question of mind over matter. If you don't mind, age don't matter.

Satchel Paige

Exactly how old is Joan Collins? We need an expert. Someone who counts the rings on trees.

Ruby Wax

Let's just say I reached the age of consent 75,000 consents ago.

Shelley Winters

My sister, Jackie, is younger than me. We don't know quite by how much.

Joan Collins

I don't know how old I am because the goat ate the Bible that had my birth certificate in it. The goat lived to be 27.

Satchel Paige

Age is something that doesn't matter, unless you are a cheese.

Billie Burke

Age only matters when one is ageing. Now that I have arrived at a great age, I might just as well be 20.

Pablo Picasso

I'm 80, but in my own mind, my age veers. When I'm performing on stage, I'm 40; when I'm shopping in Waitrose, I'm 120.

Humphrey Lyttelton

I'm 42 around the chest, 52 around the waist, 92 around the golf course and a nuisance around the house.

Groucho Marx

When I turned 2 I was really anxious, because I'd doubled my age in a year. I thought, if this keeps up, by the time I'm 6 I'll be 90.

Steven Wright

How old would you be if you didn't know how old you were?

Satchel Paige

It is a sobering thought that when Mozart was my age he had been dead for two years.

Tom Lehrer

I am just turning 40 and taking my time about it.

Harold Lloyd, 77

I am past 30, and three parts iced over.

Matthew Arnold

If you want to know how old a woman is, ask her sister-in-law.

Ed Howe

I refuse to admit that I'm more than 52, even if that does make my sons illegitimate.

Nancy Astor

The years that a woman subtracts from her age are not lost. They are added to the ages of other women.

Diane de Poitiers

I can lie convincingly about my age because at my age I can't always remember what it is.

Violet Conti

Thirty is a nice age for a woman. Especially if she happens to be 40.

Phyllis Diller

A woman telling her true age is like a buyer confiding his final price to an Armenian rug dealer.

Mignon McLaughlin

Never trust a woman who tells one her real age. A woman who would tell one that, would tell anything.

Oscar Wilde

A woman is as old as she looks before breakfast.

Ed Howe

She may very well pass for 43 in the dusk with the light behind her!

W.S. Gilbert

If the Nobel Prize were awarded by a woman, it would go to the inventor of the dimmer switch.

Kathy Lette

A woman is as young as her knees.

Mary Quant

People who say you're just as old as you feel are all wrong, fortunately.

Russell Baker

The best thing to do is to behave in a manner befitting one's age. If you are 16 or under, try not to go bald.

Woody Allen

The worst thing anyone has ever said about me is that I'm 50. Which I am. Oh that bitch. I was so hurt.

Joan Rivers

The real sadness of being 50 is not that you change so much but that you change so little.

Max Lerner

Whenever the talk turns to age, I say I am 49 plus VAT.

Lionel Blair

The years between 50 and 70 are the hardest. You are always being asked to do things, and you are not yet decrepit enough to turn them down.

T.S. Eliot

I'm 52 years of age now but I prefer to think of myself as 11 centigrade.

Tom Lehrer

The war years count double. Things and people not actively in use age twice as fast.

Arnold Bennett

I recently turned 60. Practically a third of my life is over.

Woody Allen

I have been a success: for 60 years I have eaten, and have avoided being eaten.

Logan Pearsall Smith

Here I sit, alone and 60, bald and fat and full of sin; cold the seat and loud the cistern, as I read the Harpic tin.

Alan Bennett

At the end of this year, I shall be 63 – if alive – and about the same if dead.

Mark Twain

I'm 65, but if there were 15 months in every year I'd only be 48.

James Thurber

I'll never make the mistake of turning 70 again.

Casey Stengel

It is better to be 70 years young than 40 years old.

Oliver Wendell Holmes

If it's true that 50 is the new 30, then it follows that 70 is the new 50.

Joan Collins

You don't realize what fine fighting material there is in age. You show me anyone who's lived to over 70 and you show me a fighter – someone who's got the will to live.

Agatha Christie

I'm 78. The late Ronnie Scott used to ask people their age and would respond, in his hard-edged way: 'Really! You don't look a day over (in my case) 79!' A good corrective, which I resort to when I feel sorry for myself.

George Melly

Eighty's a landmark and people treat you differently than they do when you're 79. At 79, if you drop something it just lies there. At 80, people pick it up for you.

Helen Van Slyk

With mirth and laughter let old wrinkles come.

William Shakespeare

The Seven Ages of Man

The three ages of man: youth, middle age, and 'You're looking wonderful!'

Dore Schary

There are three stages of man: he believes in Santa Claus; he does not believe in Santa Claus; he is Santa Claus.

Bob Phillips

There are only three ages for women in Hollywood: Babe, District Attorney, and Driving Miss Daisy.

Goldie Hawn

My mother used to say the seven ages were: childhood, adolescence, adulthood, middle age, elderly, old, and wonderful.

Mary Wilson

Be on the alert to recognize your prime at whatever time of your life it may occur.

Miss Jean Brodie, The Prime of Miss Jean Brodie, *Muriel Spark*

It has begun to occur to me that life is a stage I'm going through.

Ellen Goodman

Happy Birthday to You?

Two weeks ago we celebrated my uncle's 103rd birthday.
103 – isn't that something? Unfortunately he wasn't
present. How could he be? He died when he was 29.

Victor Borge

Like a hole in the head I need another birthday.

Dorothy Parker

For all the advances in medicine, there is still no cure for
the common birthday.

John Glenn

A diplomat is a man who always remembers a woman's
birthday but never remembers her age.

Robert Frost

Birthdays are nature's way of telling us to eat more cake.

Jo Brand

Birthdays are good for you. Statistics show that the people
who have the most live the longest.

Larry Lorenzoni

I had a huge party for my 70th birthday with 800 guests.
With so many familiar faces there, it was like driving
through the rear-view mirror.

Peter Ustinov

Buying presents for old people is a problem. I would rather like it if people came to my house and took things away.

Clement Freud

I was invited to Hugh Hefner's 75th birthday party but I couldn't figure out what gift to buy him. What do you give the man who's had everyone? Then I thought of it: monogrammed Viagra!

David Letterman

What would I like for my 87th birthday? A paternity suit.

George Burns

Last week the candle factory burned down. Everyone just stood around and sang Happy Birthday.

Steven Wright

Growing Old

Growing old is like being increasingly penalized for a crime you haven't committed.

Anthony Powell

Age to women is like Kryptonite to Superman.

Kathy Lette

There is absolutely nothing to be said in favour of growing old. There ought to be legislation against it.

Patrick Moorer

Middle age is when you're sitting at home on Saturday
night and the telephone rings and you hope it isn't
for you.

Ogden Nash

I am at that age. Too young for the bowling green, too old
for Ecstasy.

Rab C. Nesbitt

One problem with growing older is that it gets increasingly
tougher to find a famous historical figure who didn't
amount to much when he was your age.

Bill Vaughan

There are days of oldness, and then one gets young again.
It goes backward and forward, not in one direction.

Katharine Hathaway

People want you to be like you were in 1969.
They want you to be, because otherwise their youth goes
with you.

Mick Jagger

Only two things improve with age: wine and Susan
Sarandon.

Boyd Farrow

Jameson's Irish Whiskey really does improve with age: the
older I get the more I like it.

Bob Monkhouse

I don't believe that one grows older. I think that what happens early on in life is that at a certain age one stands still and stagnates.

T.S. Eliot

There are people whose watch stops at a certain hour and who remain permanently at that age.

Charles Augustin Sainte-Beuve

Many people die at 25 and aren't buried until they are 75.

Max Frisch

Growing old is no more than a bad habit which a busy man has not time to form.

André Maurois

When friends pressed her to carry a walking stick, Princess Alice reluctantly agreed, but she had it disguised as an umbrella.

R.W. Apple

She had finally reached the age where she was more afraid of getting old than dying.

Julia Phillips

Why do we get older? Why do our bodies wear out? Why can't we just go on and on, accumulating a potentially infinite number of Frequent Flier mileage points?

Dave Barry

I'm 43, and for the first time this year I have felt older. I'm slowly becoming more decrepit. I think you just move to the country and wear an old fleece.

Jennifer Saunders

Old age and sickness bring out the essential characteristics of a man.

Felix Frankfurter

It's sad to grow old, but nice to ripen.

Brigitte Bardot

A good old age can be the crown of our life's experience, the masterwork of a lifetime.

Helen Nearing

Growing old is something you do if you're lucky.

Groucho Marx

When the Pope Starts Looking Young

Signs You're Getting Old

There are three signs of old age: loss of memory ... I forget the other two.

Red Skelton

You will recognize, my boy, the first sign of old age: it is when you go out into the streets of London and realize for the first time how young the policemen look.

Seymour Hicks

Do you think policemen walk up and down the street thinking how old the public are getting these days?

D. Tucker

You know you're getting old when high court judges start looking young to you.

Ronnie Golden

I knew I was getting old when the Pope started looking young.

Billy Wilder

True terror is to wake up one morning and discover that your high school class is running the country.

Kurt Vonnegut

Whenever a man's friends begin to compliment him
about looking young, he may be sure that they think he
is growing old.

Washington Irving

If, at the age of 30, you are stiff and out of shape, then
you are old. If, at 60, you are supple and strong, then
you are young.

Joseph Pilates

You know you're getting older if you have more fingers
than real teeth.

Rodney Dangerfield

One of the signs of old age is that you have to carry your
senses around in your handbag – glasses, hearing aid,
dentures, etc.

Kurt Strauss

I know I must be getting old because I saw a young lady
with her midriff showing and thought, 'Ooh, you must be
cold.'

John Marsh

You know you're getting old when you feel like the day
after the night before and you haven't even been anywhere.

Milton Berle

You know you're getting older when the first thing you do
after you're done eating is look for a place to lie down.

Louie Anderson

You know you're getting old when you go on holiday and always pack a sweater.

Denis Norden

You know you're getting old when you and your partner wear matching sweaters.

Mark Schofield

I know I'm getting older because these days, before I leave in the morning, I have to ask myself, 'Did I remember to pluck my ears?'

Christopher Moore

You know you're getting old when you're dashing through Marks and Spencer's, spot a pair of Dr Scholl's sandals, stop, and think, hmm, they look comfy.

Victoria Wood

You know you're getting old when you're no longer offered a puff of the latest perfume at the department store.

Rowena Kemp

You know you're getting old when your wife believes your excuses for getting home late.

Basil Ransome-Davies

You know you're old when your family talk about you in front of you. What are we going to do with Pop? We have company tonight.

Rodney Dangerfield

Being old is getting up in the middle of the night as often as George Clooney, but not for the same reason.

Mel Brooks

You know you're getting old when you're interested in going home before you get where you're going.

Alan Mainwaring

A man knows he is growing old because he begins to look like his father.

Gabriel García Márquez

You know you're getting old when a 4-letter word for something pleasurable two people can do in bed is R-E-A-D.

Denis Norden

You know you're getting old when you stoop to tie your shoelaces and wonder what else you can do while you're down there.

George Burns

Old Age

At a church social, a little boy came up and asked me
how old I was. I said, 'I'm 76.' 'And you're still alive?'
he said.

Jack Wilson

Alive in the sense that he can't legally be buried.

Geoffrey Madan

I'm so old that when I order a 3-minute egg, they ask for
the money up front.

Milton Berle

I'm so old I daren't even buy green bananas.

Bruce Forsyth

I'm at an age when if I drop a fiver in the collection plate,
it's not a donation, it's an investment.

Ralph Layton

Anyone can get old. All you have to do is to live long enough.

Groucho Marx

How do you know when you're old? When you double
your current age and realize you're not going to live that
long.

Michael Leyden

I'm 59 and people call me middle aged. How many 118-year-old men do you know?

Barry Cryer

Old age is like waiting in the departure lounge of life. Fortunately, we are in England and the train is bound to be late.

Milton Shulman

You are as young as your faith, as old as your doubt; as young as your self-confidence, as old as your fear; as young as your hope, as old as your despair.

Douglas MacArthur

I hope I never get so old I get religious.

Ingmar Bergman

Old age is not for sissies.

Bette Davis

I don't know how you feel about old age, but in my case I didn't even see it coming. It hit me from the rear.

Phyllis Diller

The ageing process is not gradual or gentle. It rushes up, pushes you over and runs off laughing. Dying is a matter of slapstick and prat falls.

John Mortimer

Old age is like underwear. It creeps up on you.

Lois L. Kaufman

Old age is the most unexpected of all things that happen to a man.

Leon Trotsky

A person is always startled when he hears himself called an old man for the first time.

Oliver Wendell Holmes

I do what I can to help the elderly; after all, I'm going to be old myself some day.

Lillian Carter, 76

The older I get, the older old is.

Tom Baker

To me, old age is always 15 years older than I am.

Bernard Baruch

Inside yourself, you're still the same age as you were when you were 11. It's just that various bits keep dropping off.

John Mortimer

I don't feel old. In fact I don't feel anything until noon. Then it's time for my nap.

Bob Hope

Old age is when you know all the answers, but nobody asks you the questions.

Laurence J. Peter

Old age is realizing you will never own all the dogs you wanted to.

Joe Gores

Old age is a time of life when the phone rings less often, but more ominously.

Edmund Volkart

Old is when your wife says, 'Let's go upstairs and make love,' and you answer, 'Honey, I can't do both.'

Red Buttons

Old age is a lot of crossed-off names in your address book.

Ronald Blythe

W.C. Fields has a profound respect for old age. Especially when it's bottled.

Gene Fowler

Every age can be enchanting, provided you live within it.

Brigitte Bardot

Women never have young minds. They are born 3,000 years old.

Shelagh Delaney

There is no old age. There is, as there always was, just you.

Carol Matthau

Old age is like a plane flying through a storm. Once you are aboard there is nothing you can do about it. So one might as well accept it calmly, wisely.

Golda Meir

There's one more terrifying fact about old people: I'm going to be one soon.

P.J. O'Rourke

Old age isn't so bad when you consider the alternative.

Maurice Chevalier

Appearance

As I rose from my bath, I caught sight of myself in the mirror. I suddenly saw a great white sea monster emerging out of the water. This enormous sub-aquatic creature could not possibly be me, could it?

Julian Fellowes

I still think of myself as I was 25 years ago. Then I look in the mirror and see an old bastard and I realize it's me.

Dave Allen

Let us be grateful to the mirror for revealing to us our appearance only.

Samuel Butler

Sometimes I catch a glimpse of my outward self reflected in a shop window and see my mother. That old woman can't be me!

Prue Phillipson

If you really want to annoy your glamorous, well-preserved 42-year-old auntie, say, 'I bet you were really pretty when you were young.'

Lily Savage

After a certain number of years, our faces become our biographies.

Cynthia Ozick

Eric Sykes is about to be 79. He has the stretching, slowly inquiring, slightly doomy head of one of those lovely, ancient sea turtles you see on wildlife programmes.

Deborah Ross

An old man looks permanent, as if he had been born an old man.

H.E. Bates

I have reached the age when I look just as good standing on my head as I do right side up.

Frank Sullivan

Jesus! Look at my hands. Now really, I am too young for liver spots. Maybe I can merge them into a tan.

Diane, September

I swear I'm ageing about as well as a beach-party movie.

Harvey Fierstein, Torch Song Trilogy

I beg your pardon, I didn't recognize you – I've changed a lot.

Oscar Wilde

I've got enough crow's feet to start a bird sanctuary.

Kathy Lette

After a certain age, a woman should never leave the house.

Jennifer Jones

I've often thought that the ageing process could be slowed down if it had to work its way through Parliament.

Edwina Currie

I didn't want to look my age, but I didn't want to act the age I wanted to look either. I also wanted to grow old enough to understand that sentence.

Erma Bombeck

As long as a woman can look 10 years younger than her own daughter, she is perfectly satisfied.

Oscar Wilde

My looks had gone by the age of 7.

Dodie Smith

You can be glamorous at any age. It is *not* the prerogative of the young. In fact, the self-confidence of experience is an added bonus.

Joan Collins

Sex appeal is 50 per cent what you've got and 50 per cent what people think you've got.

Sophia Loren

Cut off my head and I am 13.

Coco Chanel, 60

Good cheekbones are the brassiere of old age.

Barbara de Portago

So much has been said and sung of beautiful young girls, why doesn't somebody wake up to the beauty of old women?

Harriet Beecher Stowe

No spring, nor summer beauty hath such grace,
As I have seen in one autumnal face.

John Donne, 'The Autumnal' Elegy

She had accomplished what according to builders is only possible to wood and stone of the very finest grain; she had *weathered*, as they call it, with beauty.

Ethel Smyth

I won't ever feel old, and I won't ever look old because I'm a cartoon – like Mickey Mouse.

Dolly Parton

I'm at that age when everything Mother Nature gave me, Father Time is taking away.

George Burns

When I go upstairs my buttocks applaud me and my knees sound like potato chips.

Joan Rivers

Women are not forgiven for ageing. Robert Redford's 'lines of distinction' are my 'old-age wrinkles'.

Jane Fonda

There are new lines on my face. I look like a brand new, steel-belted radial tyre.

Diana Barrie, California Suite

If God had to give a woman wrinkles He might at least have put them on the soles of her feet.

Ninon de Lenclos

One thing to be said for wrinkles – at least they don't hurt.

Betty Smith

Keep looking at my eyes, dahling. My arse is like an accordion.

Tallulah Bankhead

It's hard to be devil-may-care when there are pleats in your derrière.

Judith Viorst

I said to my husband, my boobs have gone, my stomach's gone, say something nice about my legs. He said, 'Blue goes with everything.'

Joan Rivers

Mick Jagger told me the wrinkles on his face were laughter lines, but nothing is that funny.

George Melly

When I looked at the wrinkled skin on W.H. Auden's face, I
kept wondering, what must his balls look like?

David Hockney

I'm not really wrinkled. I just took a nap on a chenille
bedspread.

Phyllis Diller

I have everything I had 20 years ago, only now it's 6 inches
lower.

Gypsy Rose Lee

Whenever I see some floozy in a boob tube I scream,
'Listen, honey, even the Roman Empire fell, and those
things will too.'

Phyllis Diller

I no longer have upper arms. I have wing span.

Bette Midler

You are rapidly approaching the age when your body,
whether it embarrasses you or not, begins to embarrass
other people.

Alan Bennett, Getting On

Fat people don't seem to age as much as thin people, not
when you get close up and inspect the damage.

Hunter Davies

After 40 a woman has to choose between losing her figure or her face. My advice is to keep your face, and stay sitting down.

Barbara Cartland

Nature gives you the face you have at 20. Life shapes the face you have at 30. But at 50 you get the face you deserve.

Coco Chanel

There are people who are beautiful in dilapidation, like houses that were hideous when new.

Logan Pearsall Smith

Like all ruins, I look best by moonlight. Give me a sprig of ivy and an owl under my arm and Tintern Abbey would not be in it with me.

W.S. Gilbert

Dress

Dorothy, was Sophia naked just now or does her dress really need ironing?

Rose Nylund, The Golden Girls

Men in the uniform of Wall Street retirement: black Chesterfield coat, rimless glasses and *The Times* folded to the obituary page.

Jimmy Breslin

Inspired by the line in Jenny Joseph's poem 'Warning' that vows, 'When I am an old woman, I shall wear purple, with a red hat that doesn't go', I started 'The Red Hat Society'. It's for women who want to grow old playfully.

Sue Ellen Cooper

Never wear grey. Wearing grey makes one feel grey. I was shown round Tutankhamun's tomb in the 1920s. I saw all this wonderful pink on the walls and the artefacts. I was so impressed that I vowed to wear it for the rest of my life.

Barbara Cartland

– Dorothy, do you think I'm dressed okay for the dog races?
– That depends – are you competing?

Blanche Devereaux and Sophia Petrillo, The Golden Girls

My mother buys me those big granny panties, 3 in a pack. You can use them for a car cover.

Monique Marvez

Caesar had his toga, Adam had his leaf, but when I wear a thong it gives my piles such grief.

Sandra Mayhew

My dad's trousers kept creeping up on him. By the time he was 65, he was just a pair of pants and a head.

Jeff Altman

I have never seen an old person in a new bathing suit in my life. I don't know where they get their bathing suits, but my father has bathing suits from other centuries. If I forget mine, he always wants me to wear his.

Jerry Seinfeld

I'm a child of the Sixties. I still wear jeans and yes, my bum looks big in them but then my bum looked big in 1965.

Julia Richardson

I can see nothing wrong with 40-, 50-, or 60-year-old men dressing and acting like teenagers. I'm an elderly man of 44 and, after a few miserable years of being sensible, I do it all the time.

Jeremy Clarkson

A sign your best years are behind you is when you slip into your first pair of slippers. They smack of smugness and a grisly domesticity.

Piers Hernu

Roll carpet slippers in breadcrumbs, bake until golden brown, then tell friends you're wearing Findus Crispy Pancakes.

H. Lloyd, Top Tip, Viz

At 50, confine your piercings to sardine cans.

Joan Rivers

– Now, if you'll excuse me, I'm going to slip into something that will make me look my best.
– May I suggest a time-machine?

Blanche Devereaux and Sophia Petrillo, The Golden Girls

Hair Today, Gone Tomorrow

I found my first grey hair today. On my chest.

Wendy Liebman

A wonderful woman my grandmother – 86 years old and not a single grey hair on her head. She's completely bald.

Les Dawson

When men get grey hair, they look distinguished. When women get grey hair, they look old. When women get breasts, they look sexy. When men get breasts, they look old.

Dick Solomon

Grey-haired men look 'distinguished'? Surely the word is 'extinguished'.

Julie Burchill

I'm so grey, I look like I'm gonna rain sometimes. And my pubic hair is going grey. In a certain light you'd swear it was Stewart Granger down there.

Billy Connolly

I used to think I'd like less grey hair. Now I'd like more of it.

Richie Benaud

I knew I was going bald when it was taking longer and longer to wash my face.

Harry Hill

Men going bald is Nature's way of stopping them having any more crap hairstyles.

> *Tony,* Men Behaving Badly

Peter Stringfellow's hairstyle is older than some of his girlfriends.

> *Paul Merton*

There's one good thing about being bald: it's neat.

> *Milton Berle*

The most delightful advantage of being bald – one can *hear* snowflakes.

> *R.G. Daniels*

I love bald men. Just because you've lost your fuzz doesn't mean you ain't a peach.

> *Dolly Parton*

Over the years, I've tried a variety of ways to regain my hair. I had shots of oestrogen in my scalp. I didn't grow any hair – but I went up a cup size.

> *Tony Kornheiser*

– Do you think she's wearing a wig?
– Yes, definitely, but it's a very good one. You'd never guess.

> *Two old ladies overheard on a bus*

People ask me how long it takes to do my hair. I don't know, I'm never there.

> *Dolly Parton*

The hair is real. It's the head that's fake.

Steve Allen

His toupee makes him look 20 years sillier.

Bill Dana

If that thing had legs it'd be a rat.

Martin Kemp

Eat, Drink and Be Merry ...

As I get older, I'm trying to eat healthy. I've got Gordon Ramsay's new cook book, *Take Two Eggs and Fuck Off*.

Jack Dee

Joan Collins says you are what you eat. She reached this conclusion following experiences in the swinging sixties and is very careful about what she puts in her mouth these days.

Mrs Merton

I'm at the age when food has taken the place of sex in my life. In fact, I've just had a mirror put over my kitchen table.

Rodney Dangerfield

Gin is a dangerous drink. It's clear and innocuous looking. You also have to be 45, female and sitting on the stairs.

Dylan Moran

I'll tell you what I haven't seen for a long time: my testicles.

John Sparkes

I've gained a few pounds around the middle. The only lower-body garments I own that still fit me comfortably are towels.

Dave Barry

I don't have a beer belly. It's a Burgundy belly and it cost me a lot of money.

Charles Clarke

You can only hold your stomach in for so many years.

Burt Reynolds

I had to go to the doctor's last week. He told me to take all my clothes off. Then he said, 'You'll have to diet.' I said, 'What colour?'

Ken Dodd

I'm on a new diet – Viagra and prune juice. I don't know if I'm coming or going.

Rodney Dangerfield

Why is it all the things I like eating have been proven to cause tumours in white mice?

Robert Benchley

Welcome to the Wonderful World of 70: The Oat Bran Years.

Denis Norden

You do live longer with bran, but you spend the last 15 years on the toilet.

Alan King

Life expectancy would grow by leaps and bounds if green vegetables smelled as good as bacon.

Doug Larson

I don't eat health foods. At my age I need all the preservative I can get.

George Burns

Age does not diminish the extreme disappointment of having a scoop of ice cream fall from the cone.

Jim Freiberg

Part of the secret of success in life is to eat what you like and let the food fight it out inside.

Mark Twain

Nobody's last words have ever been, 'I wish I'd eaten more rice cakes.'

Amy Krouse Rosenthal

Exercise

You gotta stay in shape. My grandmother started walking 5 miles a day when she was 60. She's 97 today and we don't know where the hell she is.

Ellen DeGeneres

I get up at 7am each day to do my exercises – after I have first put on my make-up. After all, La Loren is always La Loren.

Sophia Loren, 70

I exercise every morning without fail. Up, down! Up, down! And then the other eyelid.

Phyllis Diller

I swim a lot. It's either that or buy a new golf ball.

Bob Hope

I keep fit. Every morning, I do 100 laps of an Olympic-sized swimming pool – in a small motor launch.

Peter Cook

My doctor recently told me that jogging could add years to my life. I think he was right. I feel 10 years older already.

Milton Berle

The only reason I would take up jogging is so I could hear heavy breathing again.

Erma Bombeck

Go jogging? What, and get hit by a meteor?

Robert Benchley

The doctor asked me if I ever got breathless after exercise. I said no, never, because I never exercise.

John Mortimer

I am pushing 60. That is enough exercise for me.

Mark Twain

To get back my youth, I would do anything in the world, except take exercise, get up early, or be respectable.

Oscar Wilde

Whenever I get the urge to exercise, I lie down until the feeling passes away.

Robert M. Hutchins

People are so busy lengthening their lives with exercise that they have no time to live them.

Jonathan Miller

Health nuts are going to feel stupid someday, lying in hospitals dying of nothing.

Redd Foxx

Showbiz and Hollywood

I am in an industry where they eat their elders.

Dale Winton

In Los Angeles, by the time you're 35, you're older than most of the buildings.

Delia Ephron

Actress years seem like dog years and that makes me about 266.

Sharon Stone

I can't think of anything grimmer than being an ageing actress – God! It's worse than being an ageing homosexual.

Candice Bergen

You have to be born a sex symbol. You don't become one. If you're born with it, you'll have it even when you're 100 years old.

Sophia Loren

In Hollywood, great-grandmothers dread growing old.

Phyllis Batelli

Oscar time is my busiest season. I'm like an accountant during the tax season.

Richard Fleming, Beverly Hills plastic surgeon

Arnold Schwarzenegger is getting old. He's changed his catchphrase from 'I'll be back' to 'Oh, my back'.

David Letterman

Adam Faith is only 42, but Terry Nelhams is 62.

Adam Faith

I did not expect an Honorary Oscar – well, actually, I did. But not for another 25 years.

Federico Fellini

Awards are like haemorrhoids: in the end every asshole gets one.

Frederic Raphael

That so many people respond to me is fabulous. It's like having a kind of Alzheimer's disease where everyone knows you and you don't know anyone.

Tony Curtis

Music

The Rolling Stones are on tour again. They were gonna call the tour 'The Rolling Stones Live Plus Keith Richards'.

David Letterman

The Rolling Stones are on tour again. They were gonna call the tour 'Hey! You! Get Offa My Stairlift!'

David Letterman

I'm always asked, 'What about being too old to rock 'n' roll?' Presumably lots of writers get better as they get older. So why shouldn't I?

Lou Reed

The Rolling Stones are on tour again. They were gonna call the tour 'And You Thought Aerosmith Was Old'.

David Letterman

I can still rock like a son of a bitch.

Ozzy Osbourne

The Rolling Stones are on tour again. They were gonna call the tour 'We Live Through the Concert or Your Money Back'.

David Letterman

The Grateful Dead are like bad architecture or an old whore. Stick around long enough and you eventually get respectable.

Jerry Garcia

The Rolling Stones are on tour again. They were gonna call the tour 'Brown Sugar and Lots of Bran'.

David Letterman

When I give concerts, I ask women not to throw their knickers at me. At my age, I don't want to be a caricature of myself.

Tom Jones

The Rolling Stones are on tour again. They were gonna call the tour 'Under 45s Not Admitted Without a Parent'.

David Letterman

People are always talking about when the Rolling Stones should retire, but it's a racial thing. Nobody ever says B.B. King is too old to play. It's like you can't be white and be an old rock 'n' roller.

David Bailey

The Rolling Stones are on tour again. They were gonna call the tour 'Come Half-Price if You're Mick Jagger's Illegitimate Child'.

David Letterman

Times have changed. Nowadays, when people talk about the stones I want to know if they mean gall or kidney.

Cliff Renwick

The Rolling Stones are on tour again. They were gonna call the tour 'The $140 Million in the Bank Isn't Enough'.

David Letterman

Holding Back the Years

Old Father Time will turn you into a hag if you don't show the bitch who's boss.

Mae West

I don't plan to grow old gracefully. I plan to have face-lifts until my ears meet.

Rita Rudner

I see a lot of new faces. Especially on the old faces.

Johnny Carson

In Los Angeles, people don't get older, they just get tighter.

Greg Proops

I've had so much plastic surgery, if I have one more face-lift it will be a caesarean.

Phyllis Diller

I wish I had a twin, so I could know what I'd look like without plastic surgery.

Joan Rivers

Now I'm getting older I take health supplements: geranium, dandelion, passionflower, hibiscus. I feel great, and when I pee, I experience the fresh scent of potpourri.

Sheila Wenz

– I gave Maris botox injections as a gift for our wedding
  anniversary one year.
– Oh, yes, probably your 10th. That's 'Toxins', isn't it?

Niles and Frasier Crane, Frasier

Moisturisers do work. The rest is pap. There is nothing on
God's earth that will take away 30 years of arguing with
your husband.

Anita Roddick

Wrinkle cream doesn't work. I've been using it for two
years and my balls still look like raisins.

Harland Williams

Anti-wrinkle cream there may be, but anti-fat-bastard
cream there is not.

Dave, The Full Monty

The best anti-ageing cream is ice cream. What other food
makes you feel like you're 8 years old again?

Anon

The easiest way to diminish the appearance of wrinkles is
to keep your glasses off when you look in the mirror.

Joan Rivers

A woman I graduated from college with told me plastic
surgery was vulgar, that lines were a sign of character, that
it's beautiful to age. I said bull. Character is internal. If you
want to present yourself to the world with a face-lift, why
the hell not?

Judith Krantz

Everyone in Tinseltown is getting pinched, lifted and pulled. The trade-off is that something of your soul in your face goes away. You end up looking body-snatched.

Robert Redford

I call them the lizard women. They're the ones who have had so much cosmetic surgery that they're no longer biodegradable. They look like giant Komodo dragons with Chanel accessories.

Brett Butler

I wish it were okay in this country to look one's age, whatever it is. Maturity has a lot going for it. For example, you no longer get bubblegum stuck in your brace.

Cyra McFadden

I've not had any surgery. I am too curious to find out exactly how I progress every day of my life naturally. As I've always said, don't fuck around with God.

Elaine Stritch

I love my wife's wrinkles because I know where they come from. Wrinkles are the medals you've won in the battle that is life.

John Peel

How foolish to think that one can ever slam the door in the face of age. Much wiser to be polite and gracious and ask him to lunch in advance.

Noël Coward

To keep the heart unwrinkled, to be hopeful, kindly,
cheerful, reverent – that is to triumph over old age.

Thomas Bailey Aldrich

The Fountain of Youth

My recipe for perpetual youth? I've never had my face in
the sun, and I have a very handsome young husband ... Sex
is one of the best and cheapest beauty treatments there is.

Joan Collins

The secret of my youthful appearance is simply – mashed
swede. As a face-mask, as a night-cap, and in an
emergency, as a draught-excluder.

Kitty, Victoria Wood

Jewellery takes people's minds off your wrinkles.

Sonja Henie

Jewellery should be bold. Neat little pearls can add 10
years.

Joan Collins

If you don't want to get old, don't mellow.

Linda Ellerbee

To have the respect of my peers and the admiration of
young people beats plastic surgery any day.

Johnny Cash

The fountain of youth is a mixture of gin and vermouth.

Cole Porter

With them I'm Jack Nicholson. Without them I'm fat
and 60.

Jack Nicholson on his trademark sunglasses

You're only as young as the last time you changed your
mind.

Timothy Leary

It's very ageing to talk about age.

Merle Oberon

There is a fountain of youth: it is your mind, your talents,
the creativity you bring to your life and to the lives of the
people you love.

Sophia Loren

An inordinate passion for pleasure is the secret of
remaining young.

Oscar Wilde

People are living longer because of the decline in
religion. Not many people believe in the hereafter, so
they keep going.

Cyril Clarke

One of the secrets of a long and fruitful life is to forgive
everybody everything every night before you go to bed.

Bernard M. Baruch

I have only managed to live so long by carrying no hatreds.

Winston Churchill

Old people who shine from inside look 10 to 20 years younger.

Dolly Parton

As long as you can still be disappointed, you are still young.

Sarah Churchill

Whatever a man's age, he can reduce it several years by putting a bright-coloured flower in his buttonhole.

Mark Twain

At my age flowers scare me.

George Burns

If you want to stay young-looking, pick your parents very carefully.

Dick Clark

The secret of salvation in old age is this: keep sweet, keep useful, and keep busy.

Elbert Hubbard

The secret to old age: you have to know what you're going to do the next day.

Louis J. Lefkowitz

You are young at any age if you are planning for tomorrow.
I take inspiration from that wonderful Scottish actor Finlay
Currie. Shortly before he died at the age of 90, he was
asked on a TV chat show if he'd ever played a romantic
lead. 'Not yet, laddie,' he replied. 'Not yet.'

Bob Monkhouse

Humour keeps the elderly rolling along, singing a song.
When you laugh, it's an involuntary explosion of the lungs.
The lungs need to replenish themselves with oxygen. So
you laugh, you breathe, the blood runs, and everything is
circulating. If you don't laugh, you'll die.

Mel Brooks

I love to laugh. I think laughter can cure. Either the lines go
up or they go down. If they go up, that's a good sign.

Elizabeth Taylor

The heart is the real Fountain of Youth.

Mark Twain

The secret of staying young is to live honestly, eat slowly,
and lie about your age.

Lucille Ball

I don't think the trick is staying young. I think the trick is
ageing well.

Dr Thomas Perls

We must establish the idea that it is important to look *well*, not to look *young*. It is no more a compliment to say you don't look your age than to say you don't look Jewish or you don't look like an American.

Karen Decrow

– Must you leave so early?
– I must, if I am to keep my youth.
– But why didn't you bring him with you? I should be delighted to meet him.

Lady Cunard and Somerset Maugham

Maturity

You grow up the day you have the first real laugh – at yourself.

Ethel Barrymore

The first sign of maturity is the discovery that the volume knob also turns to the left.

Jerry Wright

You know you've grown up when you become obsessed with the thermostat.

Jeff Foxworthy

What I look forward to is continued immaturity followed by death.

Dave Barry

Age is a very high price to pay for maturity.

Tom Stoppard

Tony Benn immatures with age.

Harold Wilson

No one is ever old enough to know better.

Holbrook Jackson

When I grow up I want to be a little boy.

Joseph Heller

A person's maturity consists in having found again the seriousness one had as a child at play.

Friedrich Wilhelm Nietzsche

Act Your Age

The older you get, the more important it is not to act your age.

Ashleigh Brilliant

We don't stop playing because we grow old, we grow old because we stop playing.

George Bernard Shaw

I've always believed the secret of eternal youth is arrested development.

Alice Roosevelt Longworth

The ageing process has you firmly in its grasp if you never get the urge to throw a snowball.

Doug Larson

Even though I'm very old, I always feel like the youngest person in the room.

W.H. Auden

To be young, really young, takes a very long time.

Pablo Picasso

The secret of genius is to carry the spirit of the child into old age, which means never losing your enthusiasm.

Aldous Huxley

The great man is one who never loses his child's heart.

Mencius

I have the heart of a small child. I keep it in a jar on my desk.

Stephen King

I'm Not Menthyl
Malapropisms

My nan, God bless 'er, gets things a bit mixed up. She said to me the other day, 'I've bought one of those new George Formby grills.'

Peter Kay

– Barbara, didn't Elsie next door have implants?
– No, eggplants, Mam.

Nana and Barbara Royle, The Royle Family

My mother thinks a crouton's a Japanese sofa.

Mary Unfaithful

– He's autistic, Gran.
– That's nice. I wish I could draw.

Martin and Millicent Smith

Our Susan's still not had her baby. If she doesn't have it soon she'll have to be seduced.

Brenda Sneddon

Mark my words: her chickens will come home to roast.

Coral Greene

My mum said, 'I saw whatsaname last week, oh, whatshisname, I can never remember anything these days – it's this damned anorexia.'

Stephen Fry

I can't be doin' with Donny Osmond and that bunch of Morons.

Bert Fletcher

My nan was complaining of chest pains. I said, 'Are you all right, Nan?' She said, 'I think I've got vagina.'

Peter Kay

Oh, love, can you get me some of that cunnilinctus for my cough?

Edna Steele

I've got bigger fish to fly!

Elsie Mason

The patio doors are sticking again. Have you got some of that UB40?

Phyllis Amison

The doctor says I have to have a hearing aid because there's a blockage in my Euston station tube.

Joe Hadley

I don't want to see a pieciatrist; I'm not menthyl!

Hylda Baker, Nearest and Dearest

I don't want to end up in an old folk's home wearing incompetence pads. I'm still compost mentis.

Harriet Wynn

An elderly lady came into the chemist and asked for a bottle of euthanasia. I didn't say anything. I just handed her a bottle of echinacea.

Lydia Berryman

Pleasures and Perks of Growing Older

As you grow old, you lose interest in sex, your friends drift away, and your children often ignore you. There are other advantages, of course, but these are the outstanding ones.

Richard Needham

– You know the best thing about being old?
– Cardigans?
– No. Disabled parking spaces.

Anon

One compensation of old age is that it excuses you from picnics.

William Feather

One of the delights of being a senior citizen is it's easy to annoy young people. Step 1: get in the car. Step 2: turn the indicator on. Step 3: leave it on for 50 miles.

David Letterman

I can't wait to get old enough to ride in one of those buggies at the airport. Whizzing past all those poor sods on the long trek to the departure gate. It will make being old worthwhile.

Sean Needham

One good thing about being old and having a failing memory is that I can enjoy the endless repeats of programmes like *Inspector Morse*, *Murder She Wrote*, and *Midsomer Murders* because I can never remember whodunit.

Larry Simpkins

One of the good things about getting older is that you find you're more interesting than most of the people you meet.

Lee Marvin

I basically enjoy getting older because I get smarter. So what I have to say is more worth listening to, in my opinion.

Clive James

I used to dread getting older because I thought I would not be able to do all the things I wanted to do, but now that I am older I find that I don't want to do them.

Nancy Astor, 80

One of the delights known to age, and beyond the grasp of youth, is that of Not Going.

J.B. Priestley

By the bye, as I must leave off being young, I find many Douceurs in being a sort of Chaperon for I am put on the Sofa near the fire & can drink as much wine as I like.

Jane Austen

My husband's idea of a good night out is a good night in.

Maureen Lipman

One of the many pleasures of old age is giving things up.

Malcolm Muggeridge

I always make a point of starting the day at 6am with champagne. It goes straight to the heart and cheers one up. White wine won't do. You need the bubbles.

John Mortimer

Pottering is the most fun you can have in slippers.

Guy Browning

I am getting to an age when I can only enjoy the last sport left. It is called hunting for your spectacles.

Lord Grey of Falloden

The great thing about being in your 70s is, what can they do to you? What have you got to lose? Freedom is just another word for having nothing left to lose.

Clint Eastwood

As a man grows older it is harder and harder to frighten him.

Jean Paul Richter

All one's life as a young woman one is on show, people notice you. You set yourself up to be noticed and admired. And then, not expecting it, you become middle aged and anonymous. No one notices you. You achieve a wonderful freedom. It is a positive thing. You can move about, unnoticed and invisible.

Doris Lessing

Bored? Here's a way the over-50 set can easily kill a good half hour: 1) Place your car keys in your right hand. 2) With your left hand call a friend and confirm a lunch or dinner date. 3) Hang up the phone. 4) Now look for your car keys.

Steve Martin

Now I'm getting older, I don't need to do drugs anymore. I can get the same effect just by standing up real fast.

Jonathan Katz

If I'm feeling really wild I don't bother flossing before bedtime.

Judith Viorst

My kitchen linoleum is so black and shiny that I waltz while I wait for the kettle to boil. This pleasure is for the old who live alone.

Florida Scott-Maxwell

A few perks of old age: things I buy now won't wear out; I enjoy hearing arguments about pensions; my secrets are safe with my friends because they can't remember them either.

Felicity Muir

There's nothing like a flutter on the horses for a bit of excitement. Might raise the blood pressure but not as threatening as nicotine and alcohol.

Dorothy Norton

The nice thing about being old is that it doesn't affect your betting; in fact, old people betting makes more sense than young people betting. The lady in the bookie's said to me, 'Do you like having a little bet?' I told her no, I loathed it. I like to make *big* bets.

Clement Freud

One of my pleasures is to read in bed every night a few pages of P.G. Wodehouse, so that if I die in my sleep it will be with a smile on my face.

Arthur Marshall

One of the advantages of being 70 is that you need only 4 hours' sleep. True, you need it 4 times a day, but still.

Denis Norden

One good thing about getting older is that if you're getting married, the phrase 'till death do you part' doesn't sound so horrible. It only means about 10 or 15 years and not the eternity it used to mean.

Joy Behar

One of the greatest pleasures of growing old is looking back at the people you didn't marry.

Elizabeth Taylor

One of the pleasures of age is to *find out* that one *was* right, and that one was much righter than one knew at say 17 or 23.

Ezra Pound

The joy of being older is that in one's life one can, towards the end of the run, overact appallingly.

Quentin Crisp

Given 3 requisites – means of existence, reasonable health, and an absorbing interest – those years beyond 60 can be the happiest and most satisfying of a lifetime.

Earnest Calkins

Is not old wine wholesomest, old pippins toothsomest, old wood burns brightest, old linen wash whitest, and old lovers soundest?

John Webster

At 60 a man has passed most of the reefs and whirlpools. Excepting death, he has no enemies left to meet. That man has awakened to a new youth. He is young.

George Luks

We grow not older with years, but newer every day.

Emily Dickinson

The older you get, the better you get – unless you're a banana.

Anon

One positive thing about getting older is that you develop a sense of perspective about your legacy to future generations. People say things like, 'We're going to use up our Earth's resources. The Earth will be uninhabitable by 2050.' And I find myself nodding and going, 'No problem, I'll be dead.'

Dave Barry

As I move, graciously I hope, toward the door marked Exit, it occurs to me that the only thing I ever really liked to do was go to the movies.

Gore Vidal

Did you know that by the time he'd turned 80, Winston Churchill had coronary thrombosis, 3 attacks of pneumonia, a hernia, 2 strokes and something known as a senile itch? All the same, though often setting fire to himself, he still managed to enjoy a cigar.

Beryl Bainbridge

I smoke 10 to 15 cigars a day. At my age, if I don't have something to hang on to, I'll fall over.

George Burns

At the age of 80, there are very few pleasures left to me, but one of them is passive smoking.

Baroness Trumpington

– You're 86 years old. You smoke 10 cigars a day, drink 5 martinis a day, surround yourself with beautiful women. What does your doctor say about all this?
– My doctor is dead.

Interviewer and George Burns

If you resolve to give up smoking, drinking and loving, you don't actually live longer – it just seems longer.

Clement Freud

No pleasure is worth giving up for the sake of two more years in a geriatric home in Weston-super-Mare.

Kingsley Amis

The toll of time brings few delights in facing age's deadly spike; atop the list perhaps is this: outliving those we didn't like.

Art Buck

There's one advantage to being 102. No peer pressure.

Dennis Wolfberg

I feel very old sometimes. I carry on and would not like to die before having emptied a few more buckets of shit on the heads of my fellow men.

Gustave Flaubert

I advise you to go on living solely to enrage those who are paying your annuities. It is the only pleasure I have left. When I feel an attack of indigestion coming on, I picture two or three princes as gainers by my death, take courage out of spite, and conspire against them with rhubarb and temperance.

Voltaire

The older one grows, the more one likes indecency.

Virginia Woolf

I've got cheekier with age. You can get away with murder when you're 71 years old. People just think I'm a silly old fool.

Bernard Manning

At 50, the madwoman in the attic breaks loose, stomps down the stairs, and sets fire to the house. She won't be imprisoned anymore.

Erica Jong

Women may be the one group that grows more radical with age.

Gloria Steinem

I know I'm going to get old and be one of those crazy women who sits on balconies and spits on people and screams, 'Get a haircut!'

Carrie Fisher

Everything got better after I was 50. I wrote my best books. I walked Pillar, starting from Buttermere, which I'm told no fell walker of advanced years should attempt.

A.J.P. Taylor

I sometimes think that God will ask us, 'That wonderful world of mine, why didn't you enjoy it more?'

Ronald Blythe

Good days are to be gathered like sunshine in grapes, to be trodden and bottled into wine and kept for age to sip at ease beside the fire. If the traveller has vintaged well, he need trouble to wander no longer; the ruby moments glow in his glass at will.

Freya Stark

Look at everything as though you were seeing it either for the first or last time. Then your time on earth will be filled with glory.

Betty Smith

The birds sing louder when you grow old.

Rose Chernin

When it is dark enough, you can see the stars.

Charles A. Beard

I am spending delightful afternoons in my garden, watching everything living around me. As I grow older, I feel everything departing, and I love everything with more passion.

Emile Zola

The happiness of finding idleness a duty. No more opinions, no more politics, no more practical tasks.

W.B. Yeats

Sometimes it's fun to sit in your garden and try to remember your dog's name.

Steve Martin

I've always thought that very few people grow old as admirably as academics. At least books never let them down.

Margaret Drabble

A truly great book should be read in youth, again in maturity and once more in old age, as a fine building should be seen by morning light, at noon and by moonlight.

Robertson Davies

Old books that have ceased to be of service should no more be abandoned than should old friends who have ceased to give pleasure.

Bernard M. Baruch

At 76, there is nothing nicer than nodding off while reading. Going fast asleep then being woken up by the crash of the book on the floor, then saying to myself, well it doesn't matter much. An admirable feeling.

A.J.P. Taylor

Think what a better world it would be if we all, the whole world, had cookies and milk about 3 o'clock every afternoon and then lay down on our blankets for a nap.

Barbara Jordan

A nap in the middle of the day can do you good. If you wake up in your pyjamas – it's morning. If you're in your clothes – it's time for tea.

Thora Hird

I'm getting on. I'm now equipped with a snooze button.

Denis Norden

In spite of illness, in spite even of the arch-enemy sorrow, one can remain alive long past the usual date of disintegration if one is unafraid of change, insatiable in intellectual curiosity, interested in big things, and happy in small ways.

Edith Wharton

The woman who has a gift for old age is the woman who delights in comfort. If warmth is known as the blessing it is, if your bed, your bath, your best-liked food and drink are regarded as fresh delights, then you know how to thrive when old.

Florida Scott-Maxwell

Happiness in the older years of life, like happiness in every year of life, is a matter of choice – *your* choice for yourself. Happiness is to trim the day to one's own mood and feeling, to raise the window shade of your own bedroom an hour early and squander the hour in the morning sunshine, to drink your own tea from your own teacup, to practise the little wisdoms of housekeeping, to hang a picture on the wall where memories can reach out to it a dozen times a day and to sit in your kitchen and talk to your friend.

Harold Azine

I try to make each day a miniature lifetime in which I achieve something and I enjoy something.

Leslie Bricusse

If I had known when I was 21 that I should be as happy as I am now, at 70, I should have been sincerely shocked. They promised me wormwood and funeral raven.

Christopher Isherwood

Happiness in old age is, more than anything else, preserving the privileges of privacy.

Harold Azine

During much of my life, I was anxious to be what someone else wanted me to be. Now I have given up that struggle. I am what I am.

Elizabeth Coatsworth

I love having the freedom to do what I want, when I want and not care a darn what anyone else thinks. Like the old lady in Jenny Jones' poem, 'I shall spend my pension on brandy and summer gloves,' and no one can stop me!

Lilian Howard

One pleasure attached to growing older is that many things seem to be growing younger; growing fresher and more lively than we once supposed them to be.

G.K. Chesterton

The great thing about getting older is that you don't lose all the other ages you've been.

Madeleine L'Engle

From 51 to 53 I have been happy, and would like to remind others that their turn can come too. It is the only message worth giving.

E.M. Forster

Let us cherish and enjoy old age; for it is full of pleasure, if you know how to use it. Fruit tastes most delicious just when its season is ending.

Seneca

Money

When I was young, I thought money was the most important thing in life. Now that I'm old, I know it is.

Oscar Wilde

Don't grow old without money, honey.

Lena Horne

If you're given the choice between money and sex appeal, take the money. As you get older, the money will become your sex appeal.

Katharine Hepburn

Three things have helped me successfully through the ordeals of life: an understanding husband, a good analyst, and millions of dollars.

Mary Tyler Moore

If you think nobody cares whether you are alive or dead, try missing a couple of car payments.

Ann Landers

I have enough money to last me the rest of my life – unless I have to buy something.

Jackie Mason

Pick More Daisies
Regrets

– You're now 76 years old. Do you have any regrets in life?
– Yes, I haven't had enough sex.

Interviewer and John Betjeman

My one regret in life is that I am not someone else.

Woody Allen

My greatest regret is not knowing at 30 what I knew about women at 60.

Arthur Miller

I rather regret I haven't taken more drugs. Is it too late, at 70, to try cocaine? Would it be dangerous or interesting?

Joan Bakewell

If I had my life to live over again, I'd make the same mistakes – only sooner.

Tallulah Bankhead

You know, by the time you reach my age, you've made plenty of mistakes if you've lived your life properly.

Ronald Reagan, 76

The only thing in my life that I regret is that I once saved David Frost from drowning. I had to pull him out, otherwise nobody would have believed I didn't push him in.

Peter Cook

My only regret in life is that I did not drink more champagne.

John Maynard Keynes

If I had my life to live over again, I would do everything the exact same way, with the possible exception of seeing the movie remake of *Lost Horizon*.

Woody Allen

If I had my life to live over, I would pick more daisies.

Nadine Stair

If I had it all to do over again, I would spend more time with my children. I would make my money before spending it. I would learn the joys of wine instead of hard liquor. I would not smoke cigarettes when I had pneumonia. I would not marry the fifth time.

John Huston

If I had my life to live over, I'd live over a saloon.

W.C. Fields

If I had to live my life over again, I'd be a plumber.

Albert Einstein

If I had my life to live over, I don't think I'd have the strength.

Flip Wilson

If I had my life to live over again, I would have cried and laughed less while watching television and more while watching life. I would have sat on the lawn with my children and not worried about grass stains. When my kids kissed me impetuously, I would not have said, 'Later. Now go get washed for dinner.' There would have been more I love yous and more I'm sorries. I would seize every minute ... look at it and really see it ... live it ... and never give it back.

Erma Bombeck

I regret having been so polite in the past. I'd like to trample on at least a dozen people.

Harold Brodkey

If I have my life to live over again I should form the habit of nightly composing myself to thoughts of death. There is no other practice which so intensifies life.

Muriel Spark

Looking back, I have this to regret, that too often when I loved, I did not say so.

David Grayson

The trouble with reaching the age of 92 is that regrets for a misspent life are bound to creep in, and whenever you see me with a furrowed brow you can be sure that what is on my mind is the thought that if only I had taken up golf earlier and devoted my whole time to it instead of fooling about writing stories and things, I might have got my handicap down to under 18.

P.G. Wodehouse

As you grow older, you'll find the only things you regret are the things you didn't do.

Zachary Scott

A man is not old until regrets take the place of your dreams.

John Barrymore

I've never really learnt how to live, and I've discovered too late that life is for living.

John Reith

Never regret. If it's good, it's wonderful. It it's bad, it's experience.

Victoria Holt

Maybe all one can do is hope to end up with the right regrets.

Arthur Miller

If I Knew Then What I Know Now – So What?

Estelle Getty, title of her autobiography

Mustn't Grumble?

I was brought up to respect my elders and now I'm 87 I don't have to respect *anybody*.

George Burns

Been There, Done That, Don't Give a F*** What Anybody Thinks Anymore

Slogan on a senior citizen's T-shirt

I wish I loved the Human Race;
I wish I loved its silly face;
I wish I liked the way it walks;
I wish I liked the way it talks;
And when I'm introduced to one
I wish I thought What Jolly fun!

Walter Alexander Raleigh, Wishes of an Elderly Man

At age 20, we worry about what others think of us; at 40, we don't care what they think of us; at 60, we discover they haven't been thinking of us at all.

Bob Hope

I don't want a flu jab. I like getting flu. It gives me something else to complain about.

David Letterman

There's no law that decrees when and when not to whinge, but you reach a certain age – 80 seems about right – when you're expected to manifest querulousness – the coffee's too hot, the boiled egg's too soft …

Clement Freud

Bloody birthdays. Bloody women. Bloody everything. Bloody hell … Bloody footmark on the carpet now. Bloody people coming in with wet shoes …

Victor Meldrew, One Foot in the Grave

Three milk stouts – and make sure there's no lipstick on the glasses.

Ena Sharples, Coronation Street

Edith Evans bought an incredibly expensive Renoir and, when a friend asked her why she had hung it so low on the wall, out of the light behind the curtain, she replied curtly, 'Because there was a hook.'

Stephen Fry

Just because I'm in a wheelchair they think they can push me around ... I coped when a bull mastiff tried to mate with my left-side tyre.

Maud Grimes, Coronation Street

Senior Citizen: Give me my Damn Discount

Slogan on a senior citizen's T-shirt

When I was young I was frightened I might bore people. Now I'm old I am frightened they will bore me.

Ruth Adam

Many older people are not sweet old things asking for a seat on the bus; they are in many cases demanding a turn in the driver's seat.

Michael Simmons

I'm Ageing With Attitude. I am the future. We will not be crumbling ruins.

Janet Street-Porter

The Devil's in her tongue, and so 'tis in most women's of her age; for when it has quitted the tail, it repairs to the upper tier.

Aphra Behn

May your shampoo get mixed up with your Preparation H
and shrink your head to the size of a mushroom.

Anon

Nobody hears old people complain because people think
that's all old people do. And that's because old people are
gnarled and sagged and twisted into the shape of a
complaint.

Edward Albee

I refused to go on that *Grumpy Old Men* programme
because I said, 'If I go on, I will be grumpy about grumpy
old men.'

Stephen Fry

Sometimes I wake up grumpy; other times I let him sleep.

Car bumper sticker

I'm 101 years old and at my age, honey, I can say what I
want!

Bessie Delany

Menopause

The menopause is the stage that woman goes through
when her body, through a complex biological process,
senses that the woman has reached the stage in her life
where her furniture is much too nice for her to have a
baby barfing on it.

Dave Barry

– Oh my God, Saffy, darling, help. I'm having a hot flush. I
   don't believe it. It's a hot flush. Feel my skin.
– Mum, you're standing too close to the kettle.

Edina and Saffron Monsoon, Absolutely Fabulous

Someone told me that giving up chocolate would reduce
my hot flushes. To be honest, I prefer the hot flushes.

Anna Granger

I like the hot flushes. It's like being in love again without
the aggravation.

Joy Behar

Real women don't have hot flushes, they have power
surges.

Car bumper sticker

It's the menopause. I've got my own climate.

Julie Walters

I went to see my doctor to talk to him about this
menopause thing, because I don't know if I really want to
do it.

Jane Condon

A friend of mine, Norma Cowles, started The Change at
Pontins in Torquay but there were absolutely no
menopausal facilities there whatsoever. Something for
Judith Chalmers to think about.

Mrs Merton

My grandma told me, 'The good news is, after menopause the hair on your legs gets really thin and you don't have to shave anymore. Which is great because it means you have more time to work on your new moustache.'

Karen Haber

I refuse to think of them as chin hairs. I think of them as stray eyebrows.

Janette Barber

I'm trying very hard to understand the younger generation. They have adjusted the timetable for childbearing so that menopause and teaching a 16-year-old how to drive a car will occur in the same week.

Erma Bombeck

Why did the menopausal woman cross the road? To kill the chicken.

Jane Condon

At Least I Have My Health

I've just become a pensioner so I've started saving up for my own hospital trolley.

Tom Baker

The time will come in your life, it will almost certainly come, when the voice of God will thunder at you from a cloud, 'From this day forth thou shalt not be able to put on thine own socks.'

John Mortimer

I feel age like an icicle down my back.

Dyson Carter

When I wake up in the morning and nothing hurts, I know I must be dead.

George Burns

I don't need you to remind me of my age, I have a bladder to do that for me.

Stephen Fry

When you get to my age, life seems little more than one long march to and from the lavatory.

John Mortimer

At 75, I sleep like a log. I never have to get up in the middle of the night to go to the bathroom. I go in the morning. Every morning, like clockwork, at 7am, I pee. Unfortunately, I don't wake up till 8.

Harry Beckworth

Thanks to modern medical advances such as antibiotics, nasal spray and Diet Coke, it has become routine for people in the civilized world to pass the age of 40, sometimes more than once.

Dave Barry

When I was 40, my doctor advised me that a man in his 40s shouldn't play tennis. I heeded his advice carefully and could hardly wait until I reached 50 to start again.

Hugo Black

When I turned 50, I went off to have my prostate checked because I kept reading I should. Fucking finger up the arse, I can do without that again.

Bob Geldof

Be suspicious of any doctor who tries to take your temperature with his finger.

David Letterman

– How do you know which pills to take?
– Doesn't make any difference. Whatever they fix, I got.
Oscar Madison and Felix Ungar, The Odd Couple II

My mother is no spring chicken, although she has got as many chemicals in her as one.

Dame Edna Everage

Half the modern drugs could well be thrown out the window, except that the birds might eat them.

Martin H. Fischer

I don't know much about medicine, but I know what I like.

S.J. Perelman

Casey came home from seeing the doctor looking very worried. His wife said, 'What's the problem?' He said, 'The doctor told me I have to take a pill every day for the rest of my life.' She said, 'So what, lots of people have to take a pill every day for the rest of their lives.' He said, 'I know, but he only gave me four.'

Hal Roach

The good Lord never gives you more than you can handle.
Unless you die of something.

Steve Martin

You're 50 years old! Can they make a drug to help you
through all of that, to keep all your organs intact until your
golden years? No. Can they make a drug to give mental
clarity to your golden time? No. What they've got is
Viagra, a drug to make you harder than Chinese algebra.

Robin Williams

The doctor said, 'I have good news and bad news. The
good news is: you're not a hypochondriac.'

Bob Monkhouse

The doctor said to me, 'You're going to live till you're 60.' I
said, 'I am 60.' He said, 'What did I tell you?'

Henny Youngman

When you get to my age, getting a second doctor's opinion
is like switching slot machines.

James Walker

Now I'm over 50 my doctor says I should go out and get
more fresh air and exercise. I said, 'All right, I'll drive with
the car window open.'

Angus Walker

How can people complain about the length of time spent
waiting in Out Patients for an appointment? I've spent
many happy hours in our local hospital familiarizing
myself with people's ailments and afflictions.

Mrs Merton

Whoever thought up the word 'Mammogram'? Every time I hear it, I think I'm supposed to put my breast in an envelope and send it to someone.

Jan King

Everyone goes into an aeroplane or a hospital wondering if they'll ever get out of either alive.

Richard Gordon

I was under the care of a couple of medical students who couldn't diagnose a decapitation.

Jeffrey Bernard

There's nothing wrong with you that an expensive operation can't prolong.

Graham Chapman

He's on the mend, sitting up in bed blowing the froth off his medicine.

Flann O'Brien

Getting out of the hospital is a lot like resigning from a book club. You're not out of it until the computer says you're out of it.

Erma Bombeck

I rang the Enema Helpline. They were very rude.

Jack Dee

Always keep tubes of haemorrhoid ointment and Deep Heat rub well separated in your bathroom cabinet.

P. Turner, Top Tip, Viz

I'm at an age where my back goes out more than I do.

Phyllis Diller

No one should grow old who isn't ready to appear ridiculous.

John Mortimer

You don't know real embarrassment until your hip sets off a metal detector.

Ross McGuiness

Growing old brings some disadvantages, like you start having trouble with the coconut ones in Liquorice Allsorts; bending over becomes a major decision; and you can't count the number of times a day you find yourself moving in one direction when you should be moving in the other.

Denis Norden

Of all the self-fulfilling prophecies in our culture, the assumption that ageing means decline and poor health is probably the deadliest.

Marilyn Ferguson

There are many mysteries in old age but the greatest, surely, is this: in those adverts for walk-in bathtubs, why doesn't all the water gush out when you get in?

Alan Coren

We have put more effort into helping folks reach old age than into helping them enjoy it.

Frank A. Clark

My wife's aunt is about 109 years old and has a pair of glasses for every activity you can imagine – glasses for knitting, glasses for reading, glasses for doing the crossword. But she's always losing them. 'Have you seen my glasses?' she'll say. 'Surely you have a pair of looking-for-your-glasses glasses, don't you?'

Jack Dee

It's extraordinary. My mother doesn't need glasses at all and here I am 52, 56 – well, whatever age I am – and can't see a thing.

Queen Elizabeth II

My grandmother is over 80 and still doesn't need glasses. Drinks right out of the bottle.

Henny Youngman

I prefer to forget both pairs of glasses and pass my declining years saluting strange women and grandfather clocks.

Ogden Nash

From the age of 75 on, I have found my memory deteriorating and my senses getting less acute. I can mistake a reference to 'Stena Sealink' on television for 'Denis Healey'.

Denis Healey

My dad became more and more deaf, relying on lip-reading to understand people, and almost to spite him, my mother became a Moslem Fundamentalist.

Harry Hill

My granny wore a hearing aid that was always tuned too low. Because when she turned it up, it whistled, and every dog in Dublin rushed to her side.

Terry Wogan

When I turn my hearing aid up to 10, I can hear a canary break wind 6 miles away.

Sophia Petrillo, The Golden Girls

My grandmother was insane. She had pierced hearing aids.

Steven Wright

I had a job selling hearing aids door to door. It wasn't easy, because your best prospects never answered.

Bob Monkhouse

It's been said that if you're not radical at 20, you have no heart; if you're still radical at 40, you have no brain. Of course, either way, at 60 you usually have no teeth.

Bill Maher

– Dorothy, have you seen my teeth?
– They're in your mouth, Ma.
– I know that. Don't they look good today, I ran them through the dishwasher.

Sophia Petrillo and Dorothy Zbornak, The Golden Girls

My 92-year-old aunt, in hospital to have a pacemaker fitted, was asked by the nurse preparing her for the operation: 'Please give me your teeth.' 'Certainly not,' was her stern reply. She still has her own.

Roger Lines

I visited a new dentist for my 6-monthly check-up. Having given me the all clear, he glanced at my notes, then remarked: 'Those should see you out.'

Angela Walder, 72

From the bathroom came the sound of my grandmother brushing her tooth.

Peter de Vries

My father kept several pairs of false teeth, one set in a jar marked 'Best Pair', another marked 'Next Best' and a third marked 'Not Bad'.

David Hockney

My friend, George, has false teeth – with braces on them.

Steven Wright

When you're my age, you just never risk being ill – because then everyone says, 'Oh, he's done for.'

John Gielgud

You will die not because you are ill. You will die because you are alive.

Seneca

Never talk about yourself as being *old*. There *is* something in Mind Cure, after all, and, if you continually talk of yourself as being old, you may perhaps bring on some of the infirmities of age.

Hannah Smith

No one sophisticated, glamorous or interesting over 60 talks about age. So why then do other people react to life after 60 as though it were a sludge-coloured blanket which they've pulled defiantly around them crocheted large with the word 'OLD'?

Marcelle D'Argy-Smith

Old age means a crown of thorns, and the trick is to wear it jauntily.

Christopher Morley

Eighty years old! No eyes left, no ears, no teeth, no legs, no wind! And when all is said and done, how astonishingly well one does without them!

Paul Claudel

Use your health, even to the point of wearing it out. That is what it is for. Spend all you have before you die; do not outlive yourself.

George Bernard Shaw

I'm not to blame for an old body, but I would be to blame for an old soul. An old soul is a shameful thing.

Margaret Deland

No Medical, and No Salesman Will Call

Insurance

What would make life better for old people? Axe that Churchill Insurance 'nodding dog' commercial on television.

Clement Freud

All big stars of my parents' generation are on Cable TV selling things. Insurance policies to the elderly, asking them to send in $7.95 out of their last 8 dollars for a policy that will leave money to children who don't visit them.

Louie Anderson

Life insurance is a weird concept. You really don't get anything for it. It works like this: you pay me money and when you die, I'll pay you money.

Bill Kirchenbauer

There are worse things in life than death. Have you ever spent an evening with an insurance salesman?

Woody Allen

I detest life insurance agents; they always argue that I shall some day die, which is not so.

Stephen Leacock

I took a physical for some life insurance. All they would give me was fire and theft.

Milton Berle

I have done many insurance physical check-ups on people
and as far as I can tell, an insurance physical can only
determine one thing – whether or not you are going to die
during the physical.

Dr Mark DePaolis

My wife and I took out life insurance policies on one
another, so now it's just a waiting game.

Bill Dwyer

Going Gaga

They say that after the age of 20 you lose 50,000 brain cells
a day. I don't believe it. I think it's much more.

Ned Sherrin

As you get older, you've probably noticed that you tend
to forget things. You'll be talking at a party, and you'll
know that you know this person, but no matter how hard
you try, you can't remember his or her name. This can be
very embarrassing, especially if he or she turns out to be
your spouse.

Dave Barry

Remembering something at first try is now as good as an
orgasm as far as I'm concerned.

Gloria Steinem

First, you forget names, then you forget faces. Next, you forget to pull your zipper up and finally you forget to pull it down.

Leo Rosenberg

My memory's starting to go. The only thing I still retain is water.

Alex Cole

– Hurry up, Dorothy, we're going to be late for Temple.
– Ma, it's Tuesday and we're Catholic.

Sophia Petrillo and Dorothy Zbornak, The Golden Girls

'You are old, Father William,' the young man said,
'And your hair has become very white;
And yet you incessantly stand on your head –
Do you think, at your age, it is right?'
'In my youth,' Father William replied to his son,
'I feared it might injure the brain;
But, now that I'm perfectly sure I have none,
Why, I do it again and again.'

Lewis Carroll

I had always looked on myself as a sort of freak whom age could not touch, which was where I made the ruddy error, because I'm really a senile wreck with about one and a half feet in the grave.

P.G. Wodehouse, 69

His golf bag doesn't contain a full set of irons.

Robin Williams

I still have a full deck. I just shuffle slower.

Milton Berle

Spare a thought for my friend Eliza Hamilton, who was wrongly diagnosed as mentally unstable when all she was was a bit giddy.

Mrs Merton

Been There, Done That, Can't Remember.

Slogan on a senior citizen's T-shirt

– Can you remember any of your past lives?
– At my age I have a problem remembering what happened yesterday.

Interviewer and the Dalai Lama

The face is familiar, but I can't remember my name.

Robert Benchley

At my age, you learn a new name, you gotta forget an old one.

Wesley Birdsong, Lone Star

That phrase they use, 'in living memory' – as in 'the worst floods in living memory' or 'the coldest winter in living memory' – just how far back does it stretch because at my age my 'living memory' goes back to a week last Tuesday.

Alan Coren

I remember things that happened 60 years ago, but if you ask me where I left my car keys five minutes ago, that's sometimes a problem.

Lou Thesz

When I was younger I could remember anything, whether it happened or not, but I am getting old and now that I am 71 I shall soon remember only the latter.

Mark Twain

I know a lot of old people. They're all the same. They're cranky. They're demanding. They repeat themselves. They're cranky.

Sophia Petrillo, The Golden Girls

They *will* all have heard that story of yours before – but if you tell it *well* they won't mind hearing it again.

Thora Hird

My grandmother's 85 and starting to get forgetful. The family's upset about it but I don't mind because I get 8 cheques on my birthday from her. That's 40 bucks.

Tom Arnold

You remind me of a poem I can't remember, and a song that may never have existed, and a place I'm not sure I've ever been to.

Grampa Simpson, The Simpsons

– We met at 9.
– We met at 8.
– I was on time.
– No, you were late.
– Ah yes, I remember it well.

Maurice Chevalier and Hermione Gingold, Gigi

I'm very old – in my 90th year. I have a horrible dislike of old age. Everybody's dead – half, no nearly all of one's contemporaries – and those that aren't are gaga. Someone rang the other day and said, 'I want to invite you and Duff over for dinner.' I said, 'But Duff's been dead for 28 years.' [taps her forehead] That's what I dread.

Lady Diana Cooper

Body and mind, like man and wife, do not always agree to die together.

Peter Ouspensky

They tell you that you'll lose your mind when you grow older. What they don't tell you is that you won't miss it very much.

Malcolm Cowley

I am in the prime of senility.

Joel C. Harris

I'm not senile. I've been like this for 50 years. So even if I do become senile, people will never know.

Martin Landis, Night Court

On the Road
Driving

I know it's the male menopause but I fancy a 500cc Kawasaki.

Paul Nurse

They say the first thing to go when you're old is your legs or your eyesight. It isn't true. The first thing to go is parallel parking.

Kurt Vonnegut

Mr Merton is getting on in years but he's still driving. I do worry as sometimes he forgets to indicate but he always says, 'I've lived in the same road for 40 years and I think people know where I'm going by now.'

Mrs Merton

What is the age people reach when they decide, when they back out of the driveway, they're not looking anymore? You know how they do that? They just go, 'Well, I'm old, and I'm backing out. I survived, let's see if you can.'

Jerry Seinfeld

When renewing my driver's licence at the age of 83 I was asked if I would like to be an organ donor. I said, 'Who would want them?'

Constance Dean

I would think the less time you have left in life, the faster you should drive. I think old people should be allowed to drive their age. If you're 80, do 80. If you're 100, do 100.

Jerry Seinfeld

Dearest Warden. Front tooth broken off; look like 81-year-old pirate, so at dentist 19a. Very old – very lame – no metras [sic].

Lady Diana Cooper, note to a traffic warden
left on her car windscreen

The only reason I wear glasses is for little things, like driving my car -- or finding it.

Woody Allen

If money was no object the present I would like is a bleeper you can press as you enter the Ascot Racecourse car park to release a slow-moving firework enabling you to locate your vehicle. I very much regret the many hours I've spent in car parks around the world searching for my car.

Clement Freud

Grandparents and Grandchildren

Mothers bear children. Grandmothers enjoy them.

Spanish proverb

My daughter pointed out the other day, 'A granny is only a double-decker mummy.'

Jilly Cooper

We are a grandmother.

Margaret Thatcher

I can't be a grandmother. I'm too young. Grandmothers are old. They bake and they sew. I was at Woodstock! I pissed in the fields!

Karen Buckman, Parenthood

I don't like the idea of being a 'grandmother' – old and frail and the next to go to heaven. The result of this created image was that when I go to visit my grandchildren in Liverpool nobody offers to carry my case upstairs, and when someone's car breaks down they send for me to help push it.

Carla Lane

Where have all the grannies gone? I mean the genuine, original, 22-carat articles who wore black shawls and cameo brooches, sat in rocking chairs and smelled of camphor?

Keith Waterhouse

True grannies were never seen in shops. They were never seen anywhere except at funerals. They did not visit their grandchildren: their grandchildren visited them. They would not have anything to do with electricity – true grannies were gas driven.

Keith Waterhouse

Becoming a grandmother is great fun because you can use the kid to get back at your daughter.

Roseanne

Grandchildren don't make me feel old. It's the knowledge that I'm married to a grandmother.

Norman Collie

Grampa Simpson: Favourite Pastimes: napping, collecting beef jerky, sending complaint letters to newspapers and politicians, going to Herman's Military Antiques Store.

The Simpsons

Perfect love sometimes does not come till the first grandchild.

Welsh proverb

What feeling in all the world is so nice as that of a child's hand in yours? What tenderness it arouses, what power it conjures. You are instantly the very touchstone of wisdom and strength.

Marjorie Holmes

The reason grandparents and grandchildren get along so well is that they have a common enemy.

Sam Levenson

Never have children, only grandchildren.

Gore Vidal

Every generation revolts against its fathers and makes friends with its grandfathers.

Lewis Mumford

It's funny that those things your kids did that got on your nerves seem so cute when your grandchildren do them.

Raymond Holland

Does Grandpa love to babysit his grandchildren? Are you kidding? By day he is too busy taking hormone shots at the doctor's or chip shots on the golf course. At night he and Grandma are too busy doing the cha-cha.

Hal Boyle

The simplest toy, one which even the youngest child can operate, is called a grandparent.

Sam Levenson

'You're old, Nanny,' said my grandson, Tom, 'but only on the outside.'

Ellen Tate

My grandson was proud of his newly acquired reading skills and when I took him shopping he was reading every sign in sight. 'Look Nana,' he cried, 'Men Swear – they do, don't they?'

Angie Mayer

My grandchildren take me to the beach and try to make words out of the veins in my legs.

Phyllis Diller

Seeing snow for the first time, my grandson jumped for joy and cried, 'Ooh, icing!'

Alex Lacey

I was reading a book to my young grandson, Adam, about a little girl who didn't know her manners. In the story, the mother gives her little girl a plate of hamburger and chips and says, 'What's the magic word?' 'Gravy!' comes the reply. 'What *should* she have said?' I asked. Adam didn't hesitate, 'Ketchup!'

Phyl Jarski

After Sunday School, my granddaughter asked thoughtfully, 'Granddad, were you in the ark?' 'Of course not!' I replied. 'Then why weren't you drowned?'

James Potter

– Gran, you gave the baby whisky?
– Yes, it's okay. I didn't let him drive.

Jimmy Cox and Grandma, Rock Me Baby

Everyone's Favourite Grandmother
Queen Elizabeth, The Queen Mother
(1900–2002)

The Queen Mother seemed incapable of a bad performance as a national grandmother – warm, smiling, human, understanding, she embodied everything the public could want of its grandmother.

John Pearson

– I'm going to live to be 100.
– Then it will be Charles who'll send you your centenarian telegram.

The Queen Mother and Queen Elizabeth II

I've got to go and see the old folk.

The Queen Mother, 97, spotting a group of pensioners at Cheltenham Racecourse

Is it me or are pensioners getting younger these days?

The Queen Mother, 100, presenting prizes at an old people's garden competition

Horse racing is one of the real sports that's left to us: a bit of danger and excitement, and the horses, which are the best thing in the world.

The Queen Mother

I keep a thermos flask full of champagne. It's one of my little treats.

The Queen Mother

There is all the difference in the world between the patient's meaning of the word 'comfortable' and the surgeon's.

The Queen Mother after she was described as
'comfortable' following an operation

Choppers have changed my life as conclusively as that of Anne Boleyn.

The Queen Mother on helicopters

When one is 18, one has very definite dislikes, but as one grows older, one becomes more tolerant, and finds that nearly everyone is, in some degree, nice.

The Queen Mother

She is a law unto herself and takes no notice of advice.

Aide to the Queen Mother

A glass of wine with lunch? Is that wise? You know you have to reign all afternoon.

The Queen Mother to Queen Elizabeth II

– Who do you think you are?
– Mummy, the Queen.

The Queen Mother and Queen Elizabeth II

For goodness' sake, don't let Mummy have another drink.

Queen Elizabeth II to a pageboy

Don't retouch my wrinkles in the photograph. I would not want it to be thought that I had lived for all these years without having anything to show for it.

The Queen Mother

I love life, that's my secret.

The Queen Mother

Hers was a great old age, but not a cramped one. She remained young at heart, and the young themselves sensed that.

Dr George Carey, Archbishop of Canterbury

She seemed gloriously unstoppable and ever since I was a child I adored her. Her houses were always filled with an atmosphere of fun, laughter and affection.

Prince Charles

Anything that was meant to be formal and went wrong, she enjoyed. She laughed herself stupid about it. It kept us all sane. She loved to hear about my friends and all they got up to. And she loved to hear about how much trouble I got into at school.

Prince William

She saw the funny side of life and we laughed till we cried. Oh, how I shall miss those laughs and the wonderful wisdom born of so much experience and of an innate sensitivity to life.

Prince Charles

My favourite photograph of us together is a picture of me aged about 9 or 10 helping the Queen Mother up the steps of Windsor Castle. I remember the moment because she said to me: 'Keep doing that for people and you will go a long way in life.'

Prince William

– One Christmas, we were sitting watching Ali G on TV. We were laughing when my great-grandmother came in. She saw Ali G click his fingers and say 'Respec', and Harry and I showed her what to do. After three goes she had it. Later that day, when we were all having Christmas lunch, she tried it out.
– It was the end of the meal, and she stood up and said, 'Darling, lunch was marvellous – respec',' and clicked her fingers. Everyone burst out laughing.

Prince William and Prince Harry

Before I went to St Andrew's, she gave me a farewell lunch. As she said goodbye, she said, 'Any good parties, invite me down.' But there was no way. I knew full well that if I invited her down, she would dance me under the table.

Prince William

She was, quite simply, the most magical grandmother you could possibly have.

Prince Charles

Grandparents Observed

My husband and I have decided to start a family while my parents are still young enough to look after them.

Rita Rudner

My grandmother was a very tough woman. She buried three husbands. Two of them were just napping.

Rita Rudner

Grandmother, as she gets older, is not fading, but becoming more concentrated.

Paulette Alden

I was talking to my nan about Ant and Dec. She didn't know which one Dec was. I said, 'Do you know which one Ant is?' She said, 'Yes.'

Jimmy Carr

My nan has a picture of the United Kingdom tattooed over her whole body. Some people think it's weird but you can say what you like about my nan, at least you know where you are with her.

Harry Hill

'Get Off The Gas Stove Granny You're Too Old To Ride The Range'

Song title

The word 'good' has many meanings. For example, if a man were to shoot his grandmother at a range of 500 yards, I should call him a good shot, but not necessarily a good man.

G.K. Chesterton

As a child, I went into the study of my grandfather, Winston Churchill. 'Grandpapa,' I said, 'is it true that you are the greatest man in the world?' 'Yes, now bugger off.'

Nicholas Soames

Market research is about as accurate as my grandmother's big toe was in predicting the weather.

Garrison Keillor

I was watching the Superbowl with my 92-year-old grandfather. The team scored a touchdown. They showed the instant replay. He thought they scored another one. I was gonna tell him, but I figured the game *he* was watching was better.

Steven Wright

We used to terrorize our baby-sitters when I was little – except for my grandfather because he used to read to us from his will.

Jan Ditullio

I'm very proud of my gold pocket watch. My grandfather, on his deathbed, sold me this watch.

Woody Allen

My gently lachrymose grandmother had an extraordinary capacity for reliving the events of the Bible as though they were headline news in the paper.

Peter Ustinov

My grandmother was utterly convinced I'd wind up as the Archbishop of Canterbury. And, to be honest, I've never entirely ruled it out.

Hugh Grant

Helped Grandma with the weekend shopping. She was dead fierce in the grocer's; she watched the scales like a hawk watching a field mouse. Then she pounced and accused the shop assistant of giving her underweight bacon. The shop assistant was dead scared of her and put another slice on.

Sue Townsend, The Secret Diary of Adrian Mole
Aged 13¾

Oh, Grannie, you shouldn't be carrying all those groceries! Next time, make two trips.

Nathan Lane

My grandma was a tall, rather stately woman, with iron-grey plaited headphones and 1 yellow tooth in the middle of an otherwise vacant upper set. She was in her 70s when she came to live with us and had suffered two strokes since her arrival. My brothers used to say, 'At the third stroke, she will be 70-something.'

Julie Walters, Baby Talk

– Grampa kinda smells like that trunk in the garage where
the bottom's all wet.
– Nuh-uh, he smells more like a photo lab.
– Stop it, both of you! Grampa smells like a regular old man,
which is more like a hallway in a hospital.

Bart, Lisa and Homer Simpson, The Simpsons

Kids, your grandfather's ears are not gross. And they're
certainly not an enchanted forest.

Lois Griffin, Family Guy

I loved my grandparents' home. Everything smelled older,
worn but safe; the food aroma had baked itself into the
furniture.

Susan Strasberg

My Hungarian grandfather was the kind of man that could
follow someone into a revolving door and come out first.

Stephen Fry

There's one thing about children: they never go around
showing snapshots of their grandparents.

Bessie & Beulah

Parents and Children

Avenge yourself, live long enough to be a problem to your children.

Kirk Douglas

All right, since your parents are coming, I did the standard preparent sweep. Which means if you're looking for your 'neck massager' it's under the bed.

Jimmy Cox, Rock Me Baby

– Homer, are you really going to ignore your father for the rest of your life?
– Of course not, Marge, just for the rest of his life.

Marge and Homer Simpson, The Simpsons

Stay another bloody week? Over my dead body! She makes me un-bloody-plug everything at night before we go to bed – but she's got herself a bloody electric blanket on all night.

Jim Royle, The Royle Family

– You must miss Prince Andrew, Ma'am, when he's away in the Navy?
– Indeed I do. Especially because he is the only one in the family who knows how to work the video.

Visitor and Queen Elizabeth II

My parents did a really scary thing recently. They bought a caravan. This means that they can pull up in front of my house anytime now and just live there.

Paula Poundstone

My parents live in a retirement community, which is basically a minimum-security prison with a golf course.

Joel Warshaw

Why do so many old people live in those minimum-security prisons? What's with all the security? Are the old people trying to escape, or are people stealing old people?

Jerry Seinfeld

Knowing as I do Frasier's relationship with his father, when he informed me he had taken him in to live with him, I immediately flipped to the weather channel to see if hell had indeed frozen over.

Lilith Sternen, Frasier

– It seems like only yesterday that Dad moved in with you.
– Isn't it interesting that two people can have completely opposite impressions of the same event.

Niles and Frasier Crane, Frasier

– Onslow, Father's on the roof again!
– Ask him if he's got my bottle opener!

Rose and Onslow, Keeping Up Appearances

From the vantage point of his wondrously serene old age, my father contemplates our lives almost as if they were books he can dip into whenever he wants. His back pages, perhaps.

Angela Carter

As you get older, your dad gets smaller. When I went home last time, he'd practically disappeared.

Jeff Green

My father has lived so long that everything is forgiven, even his habit of referring to the present incumbent by my first husband's name.

Angela Carter

No matter how old a mother is, she watches her middle-aged children for signs of improvement.

Florida Scott-Maxwell

I am 102 years of age. I have no worries since my youngest son went into an old folk's home.

Victoria Bedwell

Children are a great comfort in your old age. They help you reach it faster, too.

Lionel Kauffman

My parents just arrived back from Singapore on the *QE2* and invited me for dinner on board the ship. 'So,' my father said, leaning back in the antique chair with a smug expression, 'enjoying your inheritance? I know I am.' He and my mother couldn't stop laughing.

Chris McEvoy

Your kids will forgive you someday. Of course, by then you'll be dead.

Sophia Petrillo, The Golden Girls

Always be nice to your children, because they are the ones who will choose your rest home.

Phyllis Diller

Twilight Homes for the Bewildered

Retirement homes are great. It's like being a baby, only you're old enough to appreciate it.

Homer Simpson, The Simpsons

The colour brochure for the Dunraven Sunset Facility showed artists' impressions of cleanly dressed oldsters watching TV and Zimmering around in rose gardens, smiling like those people you see on the Air Safety card as they slither down emergency chutes or calmly inflate each other's whistles.

Dame Edna Everage

I've got a placement as a volunteer at an old folk's day centre. They've got this 'companion scheme' where we chat informatively to the old-timers about the issues of the day, and in return they sort of tell us stories about rationing and how chicken used to taste like chicken.

Tony, Men Behaving Badly

Nursing homes. Ugh. I hate those places. All the old people want to touch my hair.

Claire Fisher, Six Feet Under

I could smell the funny odour rest homes always seem to have: a mixture of roast lamb, chloroform and little jobs.

Dame Edna Everage

My mother's suffering from advanced old-timer's disease so we've put her in a maximum-security Twilight Home for the Bewildered. Her accommodation is in the Sylvia Plath Suite. Other wards include the Virginia Woolf Incontinence Wing, the Diane Arbus X-ray Unit, and the Zelda Fitzgerald Fire Escape.

Dame Edna Everage

My First 100 Years

On 14 January, Rose will be 100 years old, and she's looking forward to receiving a telegram from the Queen. It seems a scant reward for what is, after all, a century. Come on Queen Elizabeth, give us some incentive!

Mrs Merton

I don't want to live to be a 100. I don't think I could stand to see bell bottom trousers three times.

Jeff Foxworthy

Who wants to live to be 100? Anyone who's 99.

Billy Wilder

If you live to be 100, I want to live to be 100 minus one day, so I never have to live without you.

Winnie the Pooh

Turning 100 was the worst birthday of my life. I wouldn't wish it on my worst enemy. Turning 101 was not so bad. Once you're past that century mark, it's just not shocking.

Bessie Delany

If I'd known I was gonna live this long, I'd have taken better care of myself.

Eubie Blake, 100

Research shows that centenarians are the healthiest group of people in the world. How do you think they got to be 100 years old? Because they don't get sick.

John Stark

Yes I'm 100. I put it down to 30 years of safe sex and boneless fish.

Annie Miller

You can live to be 100 by giving up all the things that make you want to live to be 100.

Woody Allen

A centenarian is a person who has lived to be 100 years of age. He never smoked or he smoked all his life. He never drank whiskey or he drank whiskey for 80 years. He was a vegetarian or he wasn't a vegetarian. Follow these rules closely and you too can become a centenarian.

Stephen Leacock

One thing that unites all centenarians is that they have wonderful senses of humour. They use it for all kinds of things, like joking about death. The thought of dying is no big deal. They've had time to prepare.

Margery Silver

I have been asked to pose for *Penthouse* on my 100th birthday. Everybody is going to be sorry.

Dolly Parton

Secrets of Long Life

– To what do you attribute your long life?
– To the fact that I haven't died yet.

Sir Malcolm Sargent

To what do I attribute my longevity? Bad luck mostly.

Billy Wilder

My father died at 102. Whenever I would ask what kept him going, he'd answer, 'I never worry.'

Jerry Stiller

– Happy 103rd Birthday, Mr Zukor. What is the secret of your long life?
– I gave up smoking two years ago.

Adolph Zukor

Good Things About Being the Oldest Person in the World:
You make *The Guinness Book of Records* without doing a
damn thing; at your 100th-year high school reunion,
you've got the buffet all to yourself; you don't need denture
cleaner – you can just call the grandchildren and borrow
theirs; you can suck at golf and still shoot your age; you
can smoke all you damn well please.

David Letterman

Bad Things About Being the Oldest Person in the World:
seems like every time you turn around that damn Halley's
Comet is back; shoulder-length ear hair; you get to see your
great-great-great-grandchildren marry moon men; all the
shoes.

David Letterman

It's a proven fact: gardeners live longer. You are young at
any age if you are planning for tomorrow and gardeners
are always looking forward, anticipating new shoots.

Mira Nair

You live longer once you realize that any time spent being
unhappy is wasted.

Ruth E. Renkl

Women don't live longer. It just seems longer.

Erma Bombeck

Scientists say that women who have children after 40 are
more likely to live to be 100, but they don't know why. I
think the reason is, they're waiting for the day when their
kids move out the house.

Lorrie Moss

– What is your prescription for a healthy long life?
– Never deny yourself anything.

Mr Justice Holmes

Ciggie-loving Marie Ellis was laid to rest yesterday – after living to 105 despite smoking nearly half a million fags. She was cremated clutching a packet of her favourite Benson & Hedges. Staff and residents from the nursing home sent her off with a chorus of 'Smoke Gets In Your Eyes'.

Sun *newspaper*

Alcohol is good for you. My grandfather proved it irrevocably. He drank two quarts of booze every mature day of his life and lived to the age of 103. I was at the cremation – the fire would not go out.

Dave Astor

I can only assume that it is largely due to the accumulation of toasts to my health over the years that I am still enjoying a fairly satisfactory state of health and have reached such an unexpectedly great age.

The Duke of Edinburgh, 80

My three rules for a long life are regular exercise, hobbies and complete avoidance of midget gems.

Kitty, Victoria Wood

I credit my youthfulness at 80 to the fact of a cheerful disposition and contentment in every period of my life with what I was.

Oliver Wendell Holmes

At 70, I'm in fine fettle for my age, sleep like a babe and feel around 12. The secret? Lots of meat, drink and cigarettes and not giving in to things.

Jennifer Paterson

The secret of my long life? Swim, dance a little, go to Paris every August, and live within walking distance of two hospitals.

Dr Horatio Luro

My grandmother just passed away, she was 104 years old. I went to buy some flowers and the guy there says, 'Ooh, 104? How'd she die?' *How'd she die*? She was 104! I told him, 'Well, it's alright – they saved the baby.'

Larry the Cable Guy

I attribute my long and healthy life to the fact that I never touched a cigarette, a drink, or a girl until I was 10 years old.

George Moore

– What is the secret of your long life?
– Keep breathing.

Sophie Tucker

If you want a long life, several years before birth, advertise for a couple of parents belonging to long-lived families.

Oliver Wendell Holmes

No one's so old that he doesn't think he could hope for one more day.

Seneca

If you survive long enough, you're revered – rather like an old building.

Katharine Hepburn

If you live to be 90 in England and can still eat a boiled egg, they think you deserve the Nobel Prize.

Alan Bennett

A Grand Old Man is anyone with snow-white hair who has kept out of jail till 80.

Stephen Leacock

I've never known a person who lives to 110 who is remarkable for anything else.

Josh Billings

Great men, men who change the world don't usually die of old age. Somebody kills them. Think of Jesus, Martin Luther King Jr, JFK.

D.H. Hughley

– You've reached the ripe old age of 121. What do you expect the future will be like?
– Very short.

Interviewer and Jeanne Calment (1875–1997)

The Oldest Swinger in Town
Love and Courtship

Your place, or back to the sheltered accommodation?

Barry Cryer

Hi, I'm Marv, your grandmother's gentleman-caller, or as you kids would say, her booty call.

Marv, Rock Me Baby

'When My Love Comes Back From The Ladies' Room Will I Be Too Old To Care?'

Lewis Grizzard, song title

They say a man is as old as the woman he feels. In that case, I'm 85.

Groucho Marx

Only flirt with women who flirt with you or you can end up looking like those old rich gents in night-clubs, proudly photographed with their arms round bimbos whose interest was clearly in the old geezer's bank balance rather than in his wrinkled and lined person.

George Melly

Hugh Hefner now has 7 girlfriends – one for each day of the week. Someone needs to tell him that those are nurses.

Jay Leno

When we were young, you made me blush,
go hot and cold, and turn to mush.
I still feel all these things, it's true –
but is it menopause, or you?

Susan Anderson

As you get older, the pickings get slimmer, but the
people don't.

Carrie Fisher

Gentleman, retired, knocking on a bit. Own teeth and hair.
Seeks lady (45 plus) for raw sex.

Lonely hearts ad

Before I turn 67, I would like to have a lot of sex with a
man I like. If you want to talk first, Trollope works for me.

Jane Juska, personal ad, New York Times
Review of Books

I was introduced to a beautiful young lady as a gentleman
in his 90s. *Early* 90s, I insisted.

George Burns

Delighted you came, my dear, and I'd like you to know that
you made a happy man feel very old.

Terry-Thomas, The Last Remake of Beau Geste

– You wrote in a story that when you reached the age of 84
  you would commit suicide. Why have you not done so?
– Laziness and cowardice prevent me. Besides, I am
  constantly falling in love.

Jorge Luis Borges

It's never too late to have a fling
For Autumn is just as nice as Spring
And it's never too late to fall in love.

Sandy Wilson

Nothing makes people crosser than being considered too old for love.

Nancy Mitford

I have almost done with harridans, and shall soon become old enough to fall in love with girls of 14.

Jonathan Swift

When one is 20, yes, but at 47, Venus may rise from the sea, and I for one should hardly put on my spectacles to have a look.

William Thackeray

Trouble is, by the time you can read a girl like a book, your library card has expired.

Milton Berle

Age does not protect you from love. But love, to some extent, protects you from age.

Jeanne Moreau

Those who love deeply never grow old; they may die of old age, but they die young.

Benjamin Franklin

The lovely thing about being 40 is that you can appreciate 25-year-old men more.

Colleen McCullough

There ain't nothin' an ol' man can do but bring me a message from a young one.

'Moms' Mabley

I think older women with younger men threaten all the right people.

William Hamilton

The advantages of dating younger men is that on them everything, like hair and teeth, is in the right place as opposed to being on the bedside table or bathroom floor.

Candace Bushnell

I don't date women my own age. There aren't any.

Milton Berle

The older woman's love is not love of herself, nor of herself mirrored in a lover's eyes, nor is it corrupted by need. It is a feeling of tenderness so still and deep and warm that it gilds every grass blade and blesses every fly. I wouldn't have missed it for the world.

Germaine Greer

I thought nobody would touch me again – not until the undertaker.

May, The Mother

– I do love the rain so. It reminds me of my first kiss.
– Ah, your first kiss was in the rain?
– No, it was in the shower.

Blanche Devereaux and Dorothy Zbornak,
The Golden Girls

Learning to love yourself is the greatest love of all, says George Benson in the popular song. I learned to love myself in the early 1980s and have never looked back.

Mrs Merton

Marriage

When marrying, ask yourself this question: do you believe that you will be able to converse well with this person into your old age? Everything else in marriage is transitory.

Friedrich Nietzsche

It's quite a romantic idea, growing old together. Sitting on park benches, feeding the ducks, leafing gently through *Saga* magazine.

Dorothy, Men Behaving Badly

Walking down the aisle together after they'd just married, Michael Denison turned to his new wife Dulcie Gray and whispered, 'Just think, darling, only 50 years off our golden wedding anniversary!' He died just before they reached their 60th anniversary.

Alan Marks

An archaeologist is the best husband a woman can have; the older she gets, the more interested he is in her.

Agatha Christie

Whatever you may look like, marry a man your own age –
as your beauty fades, so will his eyesight.

Phyllis Diller

Carol Channing, 82, star of the hit musical, *Hello, Dolly!*,
wrote fondly about her high school sweetheart, Harry
Kullijian, in her memoir, *Just Lucky*. Kullijian, 83, read the
book, got in touch with Carol, and now they've got
married. 'He's exactly the same now as he was when we
were 12,' said Ms Channing.

Amy Robinson

We've managed 24 years of marriage – with a lot of broken
crockery along the way.

Eileen Atkins

My wife and I have just celebrated our 30th wedding
anniversary. If I had killed her the first time I thought about
it, I'd be out of prison by now.

Frank Carson

My parents have a very good marriage. They've been
together forever. They've passed their silver and gold
anniversaries. The next one is rust.

Rita Rudner

I gave him the best years of my thighs.

Dorothy Zbornak, The Golden Girls

My parents stayed together for 40 years but that was
out of spite.

Woody Allen

I've been married so long I'm on my third bottle of Tabasco.

Susan Vass

The best way to get a husband to do anything is to suggest that he is too old to do it.

Felicity Parker

When you live with another person for 50 years, all your memories are invested in that person, like a bank account of shared memories. Thus, the past is part of the present as long as the other person lives. It is better than any scrapbook, because you are both living scrapbooks.

Federico Fellini

Love is what you've been through with somebody.

James Thurber

My notion of a wife at 40 is that a man should be able to change her, like a bank note, for two 20s.

Douglas Jerrold

I wouldn't be caught dead marrying a woman old enough to be my wife.

Tony Curtis

When a man of 60 runs off with a young woman, I'm never surprised. I have a sneaking admiration for him. After all, he's going to need it.

Deborah Kerr

He has a future and I have a past, so we should be all right.

Jennie Churchill, 64, marrying Montagu Porch, 41

When people ask me, *sotto voce* in surprise, 'So what about the age difference between you and your husband, Percy?' I usually shrug, smile and quip, 'So, if he dies, he dies.'

Joan Collins

You're too old to get married again. Not only can't you cut the mustard, honey, you're too old to open the jar.

Bob Hope

I was once engaged when I was 40, and I found it gave me very serious constipation. So I broke off the engagement and the lady quite understood.

Fellow of Trinity College, Cambridge, 97

Being an old maid is like death by drowning – a really delightful sensation after you have ceased struggling.

Edna Ferber

Sex

When the grandmothers of today hear the word 'Chippendales', they don't necessarily think of chairs.

Jean Kerr

I haven't yet reached the stage where I'd agree that liniment oil is a decent replacement for sex.

Stephanie Beacham

It's ill-becoming for an old broad to sing about how bad
she wants it. But occasionally we do.

Lena Horne

– There's a man on our lawn.
– Get a net!

Dorothy Zbornak and Blanche Devereaux, The Golden Girls

Let's do it! Let's do it! I really want to rant and rave.
Let's go, 'cause I know, just how I want you to behave:
Not bleakly. Not meekly.
Beat me on the bottom with a *Woman's Weekly*.
Let's do it! Let's do it! Let's do it tonight!

Victoria Wood

Pass me my teeth, and I'll bite you.

George Burns

An old broom knows the dirty corners best.

Irish proverb

My mother-in-law was on holiday in Italy with friends in a
villa situated at the end of an unlit, perilous path. A torch
was found to light the way but it had no batteries. 'I know,'
said my mother-in-law's friend, a lady in her early 60s, 'I'll
use the ones out of my vibrator.'

Janice Turner

Of all the faculties, the last to leave us is sexual desire. That
means that long after wearing bifocals and hearing aids,
we'll still be making love. We just won't know with whom.

Jack Paar

If you cannot catch a bird of paradise, better take a wet hen.

Russian proverb

The great thing about sex when you're older is that you don't have to worry about getting pregnant.

Barbra Streisand

I can still enjoy sex at 75. I live at 76, so it's no distance.

Bob Monkhouse

There's a lot of promiscuity about these days, and I'm all for it.

Ben Travers, 94

In the theatre I'm playing, there's a hole in the wall between the ladies' dressing room and mine. I've been meaning to plug it up, but what the hell … let 'em enjoy themselves.

George Burns, 82

On my 85th birthday, I felt like a 20-year-old. But there wasn't one around.

Milton Berle

I prefer young girls. Their stories are shorter.

Thomas McGuane

At my age I like threesomes – in case one of us dies.

Rodney Dangerfield

I think that Viagra and the Pill are the two most important inventions of the second half of the 20th century.

Hugh Hefner

Now that I'm 78, I do tantric sex because it's very slow. My favourite position is called the plumber. You stay in all day but nobody comes.

John Mortimer

I'm 78 but I still use a condom when I have sex. I can't take the damp.

Alan Gregory

As I grow older and older and totter towards the tomb, I find that I care less and less who goes to bed with whom.

Dorothy L. Sayers

I'm at the stage of life when I'd give up a night of wild rapture with Denzel Washington for a nice report on my next bone density test.

Judith Viorst

In my mid-60s, what I find the hardest to bear is being 'safe'. After a gym session I found myself in the Jacuzzi with a gorgeous young brunette. We had a wonderful chat, laughing and joking. But it was awful. Sitting there in her skimpy bikini, she did not see me as even slightly dangerous.

Peter Church

I have no sex appeal. A Peeping Tom saw me and pulled down the shade.

Phyllis Diller

I'm getting old. When I squeeze into a tight parking space, I'm sexually satisfied for the day.

Rodney Dangerfield

Sex and death. Two things that come once in a lifetime. But at least after death you are not nauseous.

Woody Allen

Use it or lose it.

Joan Collins

I haven't had sex since 1959. Of course it's only 21:00 now.

Tom O'Connor

My sex life is now reduced to fan letters from an elderly lesbian who wants to borrow 800 dollars.

Groucho Marx

If it weren't for speed bumps, pickpockets and frisking at airports, I'd have no sex life at all.

Rodney Dangerfield

Nowadays I reserve my sexual activities for special occasions such as the installation of a new Pope.

Dave Barry

If it wasn't for the rectal probe I'd have no sex life at all.

Barry Cryer

After 50, litigation takes the place of sex.

Gore Vidal

– Your fly-buttons are undone.
– No matter. The dead bird does not fall out of the nest.

Winston Churchill

As a young man, I used to have four supple members and one stiff one. Now I have four stiff and one supple.

Henri Duc D'Aumale

I'm going to Iowa to collect an award. Then I'm appearing at Carnegie Hall, it's sold out. Then I'm sailing to France to pick up an honour from the French government. I'd give it all up for one erection.

Groucho Marx

God gives nuts to those who have no teeth.

Arabic proverb

To succeed with the opposite sex, tell her you're impotent. She can't wait to disprove it.

Cary Grant, 72

If the devil were to offer me a resurgence of what is commonly called virility, I'd decline. 'Just keep my liver and lungs in good working order,' I'd reply, 'so I can go on drinking and smoking.'

Luis Buñuel

A medical report states that the human male is physically capable of enjoying sex up to and even beyond the age of 80. Not as a participant of course ...

Denis Norden

Sex after 90 is like trying to shoot pool with a rope. I'm at that age now where just putting my cigar in its holder is a thrill.

George Burns

Like being unchained from a lunatic.

Sophocles on his declining sexual powers

Lord, give me chastity – but not yet.

St Augustine

Work

In the days when I went to work, I never once knew what I was doing. These days, I never work. Work does age one so.

Quentin Crisp

Age to me means nothing. I can't get old while I'm working. I was old when I was 21 and out of work. As long as you're working, you stay young.

George Burns

If you keep working you'll last longer and I just want to keep vertical. I'd hate to spend the rest of my life trying to outwit an 18-inch fish.

Harold S. Geneen

I'm too old for a paper round, too young for social security and too tired for an affair.

Erma Bombeck

I am delighted to find that even at my age great ideas come to me, the pursuit and development of which should require another lifetime.

Johann Wolfgang von Goethe

Very few people do anything creative after the age of 35. The reason is that very few people do anything creative before the age of 35.

Joel Hildebrand

Like the old pro said, it's not the work, it's the stairs.

Elaine Stritch

How can I die? I'm booked!

George Burns

The Gold Watch
Retirement

I'm taking early retirement. I want my share of Social Security before the whole system goes bust.

David Letterman

I have made enough noise in the world already, perhaps too much, and am now getting old, and want retirement.

Napoleon Bonaparte

It is time I stepped aside for a less experienced and less able man.

Scott Elledge

When a man falls into his anecdotage, it is a sign for him to retire from the world.

Benjamin Disraeli

I really think that it's better to retire, in Uncle Earl's terms, when you still have some snap left in your garters.

Russell B. Long

I know how we'll end up in our dotage – my cat, Vienna, stretched across a tennis racket, and me in the local library clinging to the radiators.

Rigsby, Rising Damp

Abolish the retirement age. After all, if everyone had to stop working when they reached 65, Winston Churchill would not have been our wartime leader. He was 66 when he became Prime Minister.

Daily Mirror

We spend our lives on the run. We get up by the clock, eat and sleep by the clock, get up again, go to work, and then we retire. And what do they give us? A bloody clock.

Dave Allen

Sometimes it's better to be sacked. I hate the leaving do, and the statutory retirement present, which is always something awful like a gold watch or an engraved wok.

Greg Dyke

Musicians don't retire; they stop when there's no more music in them.

Louis Armstrong

I'll never retire. I won't quit the business until I get run over by a truck, a producer or a critic.

Jack Lemmon

Retire? Did Christ come down from the Cross?

Pope John Paul II

There comes a time when it is too late to retire.

Lord Hailsham

I'm retired. I'm now officially a lower form of life than a Duracell battery. I've been replaced by a box. It's standard procedure apparently for a man my age. The next stage is to stick you inside one.

Victor Meldrew, One Foot in the Grave

After I retired, I fished a lot, dove a lot, boated a lot – and made Johnny Walker Red about a quarter of a million dollars richer.

Dennis Diaz

What do gardeners do when they retire?

Bob Monkhouse

What shall I do now I'm retired? I thought I might grow a beard … give me something to do.

Victor Meldrew, One Foot in the Grave

I make the coffee, Barbara makes the beds, and we're right back to square one where we got married when we were 20 years old.

George Bush, former US President

My husband has just retired. I married him for better or for worse, but not for lunch.

Hazel Weiss

A retired husband is often a wife's full-time job.

Ella Harris

If I had to retire I'd probably bore my wife to tears. The commonest sight, now that people retire earlier and live much longer, is of couples walking round supermarkets, the wives filling the trolleys, the men carrying lists and saying: 'Why are you buying this?'

Terry Wogan

It's very hard to make a home for a man if he's always in it.

Winifred Kirkland

The important thing about women today is, as they get older, they still keep house. It's one reason why they don't die, but men die when they retire. Women just polish the teacups.

Margaret Mead

I don't even think about a retirement programme because I'm working for the Lord, for the Almighty. And even though the Lord's pay isn't very high, his retirement programme is, you might say, out of this world.

George Foreman

Time Flies

One day, aged 45, I just went into the kitchen to make myself a cup of tea, and when I came out I found I was 68.

Thora Hird

One day a bachelor, the next a grampa. What is the secret of the trick? How did I get so old so quick?

Ogden Nash

As I get older the years just fly by. I don't think there was an April this year.

Jeremy Hardy

Years grow shorter but days grow longer. When you're over 70, a day is an awful lot of time.

Carl Sandburg

Guinness is a great day-shortener. If you get out of bed first thing and drink a glass then the day doesn't begin until about 12.30, when you come to again, which is nice. I try to live in a perpetual snooze.

Quentin Crisp

Men talk of killing time, while time quietly kills them.

Dion Boucicault

Half our life is spent trying to find something to do with the time we have rushed through life trying to save.

Will Rogers

No matter how much time you save, at the end of your life, there's no extra time saved up. You'll be going, 'What do you mean there's no time? I had a microwave oven, Velcro sneakers, a clip-on tie. Where's the time?' But there isn't any. Because when you waste time in life, they subtract it. Like if you saw *all* the Rocky movies, they deduct that.

Jerry Seinfeld

There is never enough time, unless you're serving it.

Malcolm Forbes

Whenever I get down about life going by too quickly, what helps me is a little mantra that I repeat to myself: at least I'm not a fruit fly.

Ray Romano

Don't be over-impressed by time. Accept it, but don't kowtow to it. We should still be able to stick two fingers in the air as the diminishing amount of sand trickles through the hourglass.

George Melly

Carpe Diem

When one subtracts from life infancy (which is vegetation), sleep, eating and swilling, buttoning and unbuttoning – how much remains of downright existence? The summer of a dormouse.

Lord Byron

For every person who has ever lived there has come, at last, a spring he will never see. Glory then in the springs that are yours.

Pam Brown

Life will be over sooner than we think. If we have bikes to ride and people to love, now is the time.

Elisabeth Kübler-Ross

If you were going to die soon and had only one phone call you could make, who would you call and what would you say? And why are you waiting?

Stephen Levine

Most of us spend our lives as if we had another one in the bank.

Ben Irwin

One of the most tragic things I know about human nature is that all of us tend to put off living. We are all dreaming of some magical rose garden over the horizon – instead of enjoying the roses that are blooming outside our windows today.

Dale Carnegie

Even a great feast has a last course.

Chinese proverb

Don't ever save anything for a special occasion. Being alive is the special occasion.

Avril Sloe

Don't save things 'for best'. Drink that vintage bottle of wine – from your best crystal glasses. Wear your best designer jacket to go down to the post office to collect your pension. And, every morning, spritz yourself with that perfume you save for parties.

Geraldine Mayer

I've decided life is too fragile to finish a book I dislike just because it cost $16.95 and everyone else loved it. Or eat a fried egg with a broken yolk (which I hate) when the dog would leap over the St Louis Arch for it.

Erma Bombeck

Life is too short to learn German.

Richard Porson

Don't spend your life trying to please those who won't cry at your funeral.

Gerald Brooks

Don't wait for pie in the sky when you die. Get yours now, with ice cream on top!

The Reverend Ike

Enjoy yourself; it's later than you think.

Horace

Gotta Lotta Livin' To Do

There will come a time when you believe everything is finished. That will be the beginning.

Louis L'Amour

I want to tell people approaching and perhaps fearing age that it is a time of discovery. If they say, 'Of what?' I can only answer, 'We must find out for ourselves, otherwise it won't be a discovery.'

Florida Scott-Maxwell

Look, I don't want to wax philosophic, but I will say that if you're alive you've got to flap your arms and legs, you've got to jump around a lot, for life is the very opposite of death, and therefore you must at very least think noisy and colourfully, or you're not alive.

Mel Brooks

Let's not go out and get denture cream. Let's go to the nude beach and let our wrinkled selves hang out! We'll sit on the boardwalk and watch the old men rearrange themselves when they come out of the water.

Sophia Petrillo, The Golden Girls

Do not grow old, no matter how long you live. Never cease to stand like curious children before the Great Mystery into which we were born.

Albert Einstein

I am more alive than most people. I am an electric eel in a pond of goldfish.

Edith Sitwell

When you're young, you don't know, but you don't know you don't know, so you take some chances. In your 20s and 30s you don't know, and you know you don't know, and that tends to freeze you; less risk taking. In your 40s you know, but you don't know you know, so you may still be a little tentative. But then, as you pass 50, if you've been paying attention, you know, and you know you know. Time for some fun.

George Carlin

Life is a great big canvas, and you should throw all the paint on it you can.

Danny Kaye

Write, paint, sculpt, learn the piano, take up dancing, whether it's the tango or line-dancing, start a college course, fall in love all over again – the possibilities are limitless for you to achieve your private ambitions.

Joan Collins

Singing, fishing, meeting my close and dear friends, looking at pictures and nature, shocking a few people who deserve shocking, taking my pills, writing a book and swigging Irish whiskey. These are my ways of fending off the old gent with the scythe waiting patiently to harvest me.

George Melly

I use my increased leisure time to look at paintings wherever there is a gallery, to enjoy opera and drama at a theatre, to visit country houses.

Denis Healey

Life isn't measured by how many breaths we take, but by the moments that take our breath away.

Chinese saying

Sometimes I would rather have someone take away years of my life than take away a moment.

Pearl Bailey

We should do something that will make your heart dance once a day. If you can't do that because you're too depressed, then do something that will make somebody else's heart dance.

Yoko Ono

There were days last winter when I danced for sheer joy out in my frost-bound garden in spite of my years and children. But I did it behind a bush, having a due regard for the decencies.

Elizabeth von Arnim

I get up before anyone else in my household, not because sleep has deserted me in my advancing years, but because an intense eagerness to live draws me from my bed.

Maurice Goudeket

Most people say that as you get old, you have to give up things. I think you get old because you give up things.

Theodore Green

Develop interest in life as you see it: in people, things, literature, music – the world is so rich, simply throbbing with treasures, beautiful souls and interesting people. Forget yourself.

Henry Miller

I wouldn't mind turning into vermilion goldfish.

Henri Matisse, 80

Enjoying sex, loving fashion, having fun, decorating our homes, going on lavish holidays – the list is endless. Onward!

Joan Collins

It is a mistake to regard age as a downhill grade towards dissolution. The reverse is true. As one grows older, one climbs with surprising strides.

George Sand

You have to take time out to be old. I'm still full of piss and vinegar.

Paul Newman

If old people were to mobilize en masse they would constitute a formidable fighting force, as anyone who has ever had the temerity to try to board a bus ahead of a little old lady with an umbrella well knows.

Vera Forrester

I work every day and I want to die shouting *mierda*.

Joan Miró

I can't actually see myself putting make-up on my face at the age of 60. But I can see myself going on a camel train to Samarkand.

Glenda Jackson, actress

At past 50, I solemnly and painfully learned to ride the bicycle.

Henry Adams

I hope I have a young outlook. Since I have an old everything else, this is my one chance of having a bit of youth as a part of me.

Richard Armour

In a boat I lost 20 or 30 years straight away.

Helen Tew, 89, trans-Atlantic sailor

The only time I've ever been rendered speechless with fury was when some daft television presenter opened a programme aimed at senior travellers by asking what sort of holidays were 'suitable' for them. 'Any and all they really want to take,' is the short answer.

Elisabeth de Stroumillo

Cruising: if you thought you didn't like people on land …

Carol Leifer

Signs You're on a Bad Cruise: the brochure boasts the ship was the subject of a *60 Minutes* exposé; as you board, a personal injury lawyer hands you his business card; no matter what you order from the bar, it tastes of salt; every time you see the crew, they're wearing life-jackets; the vessel's name is the S.S. *Scurvy*.

David Letterman

I'd like to learn to ski but I'm 44 and I'm worried about my knees. They creak a lot and I'm afraid they might start an avalanche.

Jonathan Ross

I now realize that the small hills you see on ski-slopes are formed around the bodies of 47-year-olds who tried to learn snowboarding.

Dave Barry

There isn't anybody who doesn't like to see an old man make a comeback. Jimmy Connors seemed like a jerk to me until he was 40. After that, I rooted for him all the time. How could you not?

T. Boone Pickens

Golfers grow old and try to shoot their age. It must be a terrific feeling when someone asks your age and you can say, 'Par.'

The Pittsburgh Post

The older you get, the stronger the wind gets – and it's always in your face.

Jack Nicklaus

You're never too old. A person of 60 can grow as much as a child of 6. Michelangelo did some of his best paintings when past 80; George Bernard Shaw was still writing plays at 90; Grandma Moses didn't even begin painting until she was 79.

Maxwell Naltz

I don't want to get to the end of my life and find that I lived just the length of it. I want to have lived the width of it as well.

Diane Ackerman

Life is either a daring adventure, or nothing.

Helen Keller

Dance as if no one were watching, sing as if no one were listening, and live every day as if it were your last.

Tish Provest

Do not go gently into that good night,
Old age should burn and rage at close of day …

Dylan Thomas

There is sleeping enough in the grave.

Irish saying

A Quiet Life

I once wanted to save the world. Now I just want to leave the room with some dignity.

Lotus Weinstock

As I grow old, I find myself less and less inclined to take the stairs two at a time.

Bernard Baruch

I turn 70 this year and all of a sudden the horizon that once seemed far away looms right there in front of you. You feel an irresistible urge to slow down, to take your foot off the accelerator, touch it to the brake – gently, but surely – and start negotiating yourself out of the fast lane.

Bill Moyers, former White House Press Secretary

I am 72 years of age, at which period there come over one a shameful love of ease and repose, common to dogs, horses, clergymen and even to *Edinburgh Reviewers*. Then an idea comes across me that I am entitled to 5 or 6 years of quiet before I die.

Rev. Sydney Smith

Even under a harsh God, one is entitled to serenity in old age.

Albert Outler

What is wrong with settling down with a good book into a rocking chair by the fireside, wearing a comfy pair of slippers if that is what makes you happy?

Eloise Pagett

I love this time of day. When I'm sitting here in my own little home, with my own wonderful little hubby, and we talk about issues of the day and discuss world affairs and generally just snuggle.

Mavis Wilton, Coronation Street

I used to have a sign over my computer that read, 'Old Dogs Can Learn New Tricks', but lately I sometimes ask myself how many more tricks I *want* to learn. Wouldn't it be easier to be outdated?

Ram Dass

If old age in the shape of waning strength says to me often, 'Thou shalt not!', so do my years smile upon me and say to me, 'Thou needst not!'

Mary Vorse

It's only natural that a person becomes quieter as they grow older. They've got more to keep quiet about.

Samuel Butler

One's first step to wisdom is to question everything – and one's last is to come to terms with everything.

Georg Christoph Lichtenberg

Growing older, I have lost the need to be political, which means, in this country, the need to be left. I am driven into grudging toleration of the Conservative Party because it is the party of non-politics, of resistance to politics.

Kingsley Amis

When one has reached 81, one likes to sit back and let the world turn by itself, without trying to push it.

Sean O'Casey

The members seated in the Pavilion at the Test Match declined to join in the Mexican Wave. Well, when you get to a certain age, every time you just get out of your chair, it's a bit of an adventure.

Henry Blofeld

Old men are dangerous; it doesn't matter to them what is going to happen to the world.

George Bernard Shaw

Rest is not idleness, and to lie sometimes on the grass on a summer day listening to the murmur of water, or watching the clouds float across the sky, is hardly a waste of time.

John Lubbock

I shall be 70 in two months' time and feel exactly as I did when I was 20. I was idle and indolent then, and little has changed in the past 50 years except that perhaps now I am better at getting away with it.

Arnold Thomson

Mind-Lift

When it comes to staying young, a mind-lift beats a face-lift any day.

Marty Bucella

In my old age there is a coming into flower. My body wanes; mind waxes.

Victor Hugo

Although I am 92, my brain is 30 years old.

Alfred Eisenstaedt

Anyone who stops learning is old, whether at 20 or 80. Anyone who keeps learning stays young. The greatest thing in life is to keep your mind young.

Henry Ford

We get too soon old, and too late smart.

Dutch

Silver Surfers
Technology

– Mother, are you still on the computer?
– Yes, dear. Sometimes you get into a porn loop and just
can't get out.

Edina Monsoon and her mother, Absolutely Fabulous

Here I sit, a modern Werther Original. Not telling dusty
fairy stories to my 4-year-old and feeding him teeth-rotting
toffees but teaching him how to work my computer so that
one day soon he can teach me things.

Peter Preston

A great way to meet the opposite sex when you're older is
on the Internet, a good reason to learn to use a computer.
The Internet is 70 per cent men, so the odds are definitely
in a woman's favour for finding a guy.

Joan Rivers

My nan said, 'What do you mean when you say the
computer went down on you?'

Joseph Longthorne

Experts agree that the best type of computer for your
individual needs is one that comes on the market about 2
days after you actually purchase some other computer.

Dave Barry

During my 87 years, I have witnessed a whole succession of technological revolutions; but none of them has done away with the need for character in the individual, or the ability to think.

Bernard Baruch

Age and Youth

When I was young there was no respect for the young, and now that I am old there is no respect for the old. I missed out coming and going.

J.B. Priestley

I'm quite happy about growing older. Who wants to be young? Being 18 is like visiting Russia. You're glad you've had the experience but you'd never want to repeat it.

Barbara Cartland

When I see a young girl I view her with the same pity that she views me with.

Lilli Palmer

We are happier in many ways when we are old than when we are young. The young sow wild oats, the old grow sage.

Winston Churchill

Young people know the rules. Old people know the exceptions.

Oliver Wendell Holmes

I've got things in my refrigerator older than you.

Lee Trevino to Tiger Woods

Old people have one advantage compared with young ones. They have been young themselves, and young people haven't been old.

Lord Longford

Youth is something very new: 20 years ago no one mentioned it.

Coco Chanel, 1971

There's one thing I have over any 21-year-old: a proud history of accumulated neuroses.

Ray Romano

Never have I enjoyed youth so thoroughly as I have in my old age.

George Santayana

Young men wish for love, money, and health. One day, they'll say health, money, and love.

Paul Géraldy

Age is not an accomplishment, and youth is not a sin.

Robert Heinlen

This is a youth-orientated society, and the joke is on them because youth is a disease from which we all recover.

Dorothy Fuldheim

All sorts of allowances are made for the illusions of youth; and none for the disenchantments of old age.

Robert Louis Stevenson

I never dared to be radical when young for fear it would make me conservative when old.

Robert Frost

Old age realizes the dreams of youth. Look at Dean Swift: in his youth he built an asylum for the insane; in his old age he was himself an inmate.

Søren Kierkegaard

If youth but knew; if age but could.

Henri Estienne

The belief that youth is the happiest time of life is founded on a fallacy. The happiest person is the person who thinks the most interesting thoughts, and we grow happier as we grow older.

William Phelps

When you are 92 and you say, 'When I was 74,' it's almost like saying, 'When I was young!'

Ernest Waring

Old and young, we are all on our last cruise.

Robert Louis Stevenson

Mind the Gap
The Generation Gap

Blessed are the young for they shall inherit the national debt.

Herbert Hoover

Every generation supposes that the world was simpler for the one before it.

Eleanor Roosevelt

Your modern teenager is not about to listen to advice from an old person, defined as a person who remembers when there was no Velcro.

Dave Barry

I used to call anyone over the age of 35, R.F.C. – Ready For Chrysanthemums.

Brigitte Bardot

My son does not appreciate classical musicians such as the Rolling Stones; he is more into bands with names like 'Heave' and 'Squatting Turnips'.

Dave Barry

The denunciation of the young is a necessary part of the hygiene of older people, and greatly assists the circulation of their blood.

Logan Pearsall Smith

The reason people blame things on the previous generation is that there's only one other choice.

Doug Larson

Parents often talk about the younger generation as if they didn't have anything to do with it.

Haim Ginott

There is nothing wrong with the younger generation which the older generation did not outgrow.

Gail Hammond

In case you're worried about what's going to become of the younger generation, it's going to grow up and start worrying about the younger generation.

Roger Allen

The Good Old Days?

In my old age I find no pleasure save in the memories which I have of the past.

Giacomo Casanova

We have all got our 'good old days' tucked away inside our hearts and we return to them in dreams like cats to favourite armchairs.

Brian Carter

I have liked remembering almost as much as I have liked living.

William Maxwell

Reread all the letters you've kept over the years – the wonderful thing is, you won't have to answer them.

Thora Hird

When we recall the past, we usually find that it is the simplest things – not the great occasions – that in retrospect give off the greatest glory of happiness.

Bob Hope

In July, when I bury my nose in a hazel bush, I feel 15 years old again. It's lovely! It smells of love!

Camille Corot

One of the oddest things in life, I think, is the things one remembers.

Agatha Christie

In memory, everything seems to happen to music.

Tennessee Williams

– Do you remember the minuet?
– Dahling, I can't even remember the men I *slept* with!

Tallulah Bankhead

I never saw a banana till I was 14. I was immediately sick after eating it and haven't touched one since.

Enid Bray

I remember when the wireless was something useful. In my day you could warm your hands on the wireless and listen to Terry Wogan. Nowadays all you can do is listen to Wogan.

Paula Brett

In my day, there were things that were done, and things that were not done, and there was even a way of doing things that were not done.

Peter Ustinov

In my day, a juvenile delinquent was a kid who owed tuppence on an overdue library book.

Max Bygraves

When you are about 35 years old, something terrible always happens to music.

Steve Race

Call those pants? I can remember when pants were pants. You wore them for 20 years, then you cut them down for pan scrubs.

Old Bag, Victoria Wood

In my day, men wore driving gloves, women stayed married, and curry had raisins in it.

Swiss Toni, The Fast Show

When I was a child, we took it in turns to have a bath: first the kids, then the whippets, then Granddad.

Ken Dodd

We couldn't afford a proper bath. We just had a pan of water and we'd wash down as far as possible and we'd wash up as far possible. Then, when somebody'd clear the room, we'd wash possible.

Dolly Parton

The older a man gets, the farther he had to walk to school as a boy.

Henry Brightman

In my day, no one had cars. If you wanted to get run over, you'd to catch a bus to the main road … And we didn't do all this keep-fit. We got our exercise lowering coffins out of upstairs windows.

Old Bag, Victoria Wood

Nostalgia is a longing for something you couldn't stand anymore.

Fibber McGee

People say, oh, it's not like the good old days. When were the good old days? In 1900 your doctor was also your barber. 'Say, will you take a little off the sides when you take out my spleen?'

Joe Ditzel

As lousy as things are now, tomorrow they will be somebody's good old days.

Gerald Barzan

If one day you're going to be able to look back on something and laugh about it, you might as well laugh about it now.

Marie Osmond

Always have old memories and young hopes.

Arsene Houssaye

Life

Life is a funny thing that happens to you on the way to the grave.

Quentin Crisp

Life is a moderately good play with a badly written third act.

Truman Capote

Life is a marathon in which you reserve the sprint for the end. Mentally I pace myself. I have got an energy bank account and I can't afford to be overdrawn.

Peter Ustinov

Life can only be understood backwards, but it must be lived forwards.

Søren Kierkegaard

You only live once, but if you do it right, once is enough.

Mae West

Life is rather like opening a tin of sardines. We're all of us looking for the key.

Alan Bennett

What if the hokey cokey really is what it's all about?

Bob Monkhouse

If logic tells you that life is a meaningless accident, don't give up on life. Give up on logic.

Shira Milgrom

There are only 2 ways to live your life. One is as though nothing is a miracle. The other is as though everything is a miracle.

Albert Einstein

All life is a failure in the end. The thing is to get sport out of trying.

Sir Francis Chichester

I love living. I have sometimes been wildly, despairingly, acutely miserable, racked with sorrow, but through it all, I still know quite certainly that just to be alive is a grand thing.

Agatha Christie

That it will never come again is what makes life so sweet.

Emily Dickinson

Experience

Experience is the one thing you have plenty of when you're too old to get the job.

Laurence J. Peter

Experience is the name everyone gives to their mistakes.

Oscar Wilde

Experience is a comb life gives you after you lose your hair.

Judith Stern

A prune is an experienced plum.

John Trattner

I have learned throughout my life as a composer chiefly through my mistakes and pursuits of false assumptions, not by my exposure to wisdom and founts of knowledge.

Igor Stravinsky

We learn from experience that man never learns from experience.

George Bernard Shaw

If we could sell our experiences for what they cost us, we'd all be millionaires.

Abigail Van Buren

Good and Bad

Old age is a great trial. One has to be so damned *good*!

May Sarton

When you are younger you get blamed for crimes you never committed and when you're older you begin to get credit for virtues you never possessed. It evens itself out.

I.F. Stone

Basil Blackwell said that he had certainly been depraved by the book, *Last Exit to Brooklyn*, but as he was in his 80s at the time the matter didn't seem to be of great practical significance.

John Mortimer

What on earth has happened to outrage? There is a hell of a lot in this life to be furious about – and not just things affecting older people – and yet everybody seems to be taking it all so easy. We want more outrage.

Margaret Simey

Old age is an excellent time for outrage. My goal is to say or do at least one outrageous thing every week.

Maggie Kuhn

An 80-year-old man sentenced to 10 years in jail, said to the judge, 'I'll never live that long.' The judge replied, 'Well, do the best you can.'

Anon

Years and sins are always more than acknowledged.

Italian proverb

One should never make one's debut with a scandal; one should reserve that to give interest in one's old age.

Oscar Wilde

Old men like giving good advice to console themselves for no longer being able to set bad examples.

La Rochefoucauld

Don't worry about avoiding temptation – as you grow older, it starts avoiding you.

Michael Ford

Thank You for Being a Friend
Friendship

As life goes on, don't you find that all you need is about two real friends, a regular supply of books, and a Peke?

P.G. Wodehouse

We need old friends to help us grow old and new friends to help us stay young.

Letty Cottin Pogrebin

One consolation of ageing is realizing that while you have been growing old your friends haven't been standing still in the matter either.

Clare Boothe Luce

The mere process of growing old together will make our slightest acquaintances seem like bosom-friends.

Logan Pearsall Smith

When you're 50 you start thinking about things you haven't thought about before. I used to think getting old was about vanity – but actually it's about losing people you love. Getting wrinkles is trivial.

Joyce Carol Oates

If I had any decency, I'd be dead. Most of my friends are.

Dorothy Parker

The loss of friends is a tax on age!

Ninon de Lenclos

I don't have a warm personal enemy left. They've all died off. I miss them terribly because they helped define me.

Clare Boothe Luce

My only profile of heaven is a large blue sky ... larger than the biggest I have seen in June – and in it are my friends – every one of them.

Emily Dickinson

All my friends are dead. They're all in heaven now and they're all up there mingling with one another. By now, they are starting to wonder if I might have gone to the other place.

Teresa Platt

Going, Going, Gone!
Death

Why did I not do more in my life, I ask myself, as I read the obituaries of the people who have crammed their lives with 'doing' while I have wasted great chunks of mine dreaming?

Mary Wesley

My old mam read the obituary column every day but she could never understand how people always die in alphabetical order.

Frank Carson

I have never killed a man, but I have read many obituaries with great pleasure.

Clarence Darrow

When I get in a taxi, the first thing they say is, 'Hello Eric, I thought you were dead.'

Eric Sykes

I have been dead for two years, but I don't choose to have it known.

Lord Chesterfield

There are so many ways of dying, it is astonishing that any of us choose old age.

Beryl Bainbridge

There are worse things to die of than old age.

Clive James

How young can you die of old age?

Steven Wright

Hope I die before I get old.

Pete Townshend

I want to die young at an advanced age.

Max Lerner

Statistics tell us that Audrey Hepburn died young. What no statistics can show us is that she would have died young at any age.

Peter Ustinov

Jesus died too soon. If he had lived to my age he would have repudiated his doctrine.

Friedrich Nietzsche, 48

I don't mind dying. Trouble is, you feel so bloody stiff the next day.

George Axelrod

It seems like the only two times they pronounce you anything in life is when they pronounce you 'man and wife' or 'dead on arrival'.

Dennis Miller

– When we die, certain things keep growing – your fingernails, the hair on your head, the hair on your chest…

– Not the hair on *my* chest!

– My dear, you give up hope too easily.

Lawrence Olivier and Edith Evans

For three days after death, hair and fingernails continue to grow but phone calls taper off.

Johnny Carson

Better take my photograph now, dear – I'm 80, I might die at lunch.

Lady Diana Cooper to a magazine photographer

At a formal dinner party, the person nearest death should always be seated closest to the bathroom.

George Carlin

I am ready to meet my Maker. Whether my Maker is ready for the ordeal of meeting me is another matter.

Winston Churchill, on his 75th birthday

My family has a propensity – it must be in our genes – for dropping dead. Here one minute, gone the next. Neat. I pray that I have inherited this gene.

Mary Wesley

– How would you like to die?

– At the end of a sentence.

Interviewer and Peter Ustinov

My dream is to die in a tub of ice cream, with Mel Gibson.

Joan Rivers

Let me die eating ortolans to the sound of soft music.

Benjamin Disraeli

I want Death to find me planting my cabbages.

Michel de Montaigne

I shall not die of a cold. I shall die of having lived.

Willa Cather

Errol Flynn died on a 70-foot yacht with a 17-year-old girl. My husband's always wanted to go that way, but he's going to settle for a 17-footer and a 70-year-old.

Mrs Walter Cronkite

– I've decided I want to be cremated.
– C'mon then, Nana, get your coat ...

Alfie and Nana Moon, EastEnders

Where would I like my ashes scattered? I don't know. Surprise me.

Bob Hope

I told my wife I want to be cremated. She's planning a barbecue.

Rodney Dangerfield

If there wasn't death, I think you couldn't go on.

Stevie Smith

It was Death – possibly the only dinner guest more unwelcome than Sidney Poitier.

Kinky Friedman

Death is nature's way of saying, 'Your table is ready.'

Robin Williams

Dying is a very dull, dreary affair. And my advice to you is to have nothing whatever to do with it.

Somerset Maugham

I'm not afraid to die, honey. In fact I'm kinda looking forward to it. I know that the Lord has his arms wrapped around this big, fat sparrow.

Ethel Waters

I'm not afraid of death. It's the stake one puts up in order to play the game of life.

Jean Giraudoux

It's not that I'm afraid to die. I just don't want to be there when it happens.

Woody Allen

Dying is no big deal. The least of us will manage that. Living is the trick. My life has been strawberries in the wintertime, and you can't ask for more than that.

Red Smith

What a simple thing death is, just as simple as the falling of an autumn leaf.

Vincent Van Gogh

Under the soil, I'll become part of a daisy or a cowslip. To return to the earth will be a kind of reincarnation.

Joan Bakewell

Life is a great surprise. I do not see why death should not be an even greater one.

Vladimir Nabokov

At my age, I'm often asked if I'm frightened of death and my reply is always, I can't remember being frightened of birth.

Peter Ustinov

To die will be an awfully big adventure.

J.M. Barrie

Dying is one of the few things that can be done just as easily lying down.

Woody Allen

I'm dying but otherwise I'm in very good health.

Edith Sitwell

Life is too short but it would be absolutely awful if it were too long.

Peter Ustinov

We should be more like elephants. When they are dying they creep off and get out of the way.

Mary Warnock, 80

Like a prisoner awaiting his release, like a schoolboy when the end of term is near, like a migrant bird ready to fly south … I long to be gone.

Malcolm Muggeridge

– When my time comes, I sure want somebody to put me out of my misery if something tragic happens, like I get a fatal illness or I've lost my looks.
– Just tell us when, Blanche.

Blanche Devereaux and Dorothy Zbornak, The Golden Girls

If I'm ever stuck on a respirator or a life support system I definitely want to be unplugged. But not until I'm down to a size 8.

Henriette Mantel

Euthanasia is a way of putting old people out of their family's misery.

Mike Barfield

My husband died aged 79. He led a wonderful life and never suffered unless I wanted him to.

Suzanne Sugarbaker, Women of the House

My husband died while we were making love. I thought it was funny when he kept saying, 'I'm going! … I'm going!'

Rose Nylund, The Golden Girls

On Sunday 5 April 1998, following a courageous fight for life, Catherine Thomas (née Holder) surrounded by family, died at home – and she's bloody annoyed.

Obituary notice, Cardiff newspaper

When I told my daughter that Edith Evans had died, she said, 'I don't believe it. She's not the type.'

Bryan Forbes

George Gershwin died on 11 July 1937, but I don't have to believe it if I don't want to.

John O'Hara

There is something about a poet which leads us to believe that he died, in many cases, as long as 20 years before his birth.

James Thurber

The man who invented the hokey cokey has died. His funeral was a strange affair. First, they put his left leg in ...

Al Ferrera

Martin Levine has passed away at the age of 75. Mr Levine had owned a movie theatre chain in New York. The funeral will be held on Thursday at 2.15, 4.20, 6.30, 8.40, and 10.50.

David Letterman

The inventor of Crest passed away. Four out of five dentists came to the funeral.

Jay Leno

Funeral services were held this week for 82-year-old chewing gum magnate Philip K. Wrigley. In keeping with his last request, Wrigley's remains will be stuck to the bottom of a luncheonette counter.

Jane Curtin

The Chairman of MORI polls has died. He'll be missed by 80 per cent of his family and 35 per cent of his friends.

Craig Kilborn

The Lucky Stiff Funeral Home: We Put the Fun into Funeral.

The Simpsons

They say such lovely things about people at their funerals, it's a shame I'm going to miss mine by just a few days.

Bob Monkhouse

Why is it that we rejoice at a birth and grieve at a funeral? Is it because we are not the person involved?

Mark Twain

This is the last time I will take part as an amateur.

Daniel François Esprit Auber, 76, at a funeral

There's nothing like a morning funeral for sharpening the appetite for lunch.

Arthur Marshall

I always thought I'd be the first to go ... Weren't they lovely, them vol au vent. What was in 'em? It was a sort of mushroomy thing. Hey, can I have them when I go, Barbara?

Nana, The Royle Family

I used to hate weddings – all those old dears poking me in the stomach and saying, 'You're next.' But they stopped all that when I started doing the same to them at funerals.

Gail Flynn

In Liverpool, the difference between a funeral and a wedding is one less drunk.

Paul O'Grady

When you're my age, you worry about 2 things – one is when a woman says, 'Let's do it again, right now,' and the other is, 'Who's going to come to my funeral?'

Alan King

Always go to other people's funerals, otherwise they won't come to yours.

Yogi Berra

No matter how rich you become, how famous or powerful, when you die the size of your funeral will still pretty much depend on the weather.

Michael Pritchard

In the city a funeral is just an interruption in the traffic; in the country it is a form of popular entertainment.

George Ade

A stooped old man stood, deep in thought, watching the funeral procession pass by. I whispered to him, 'Who died?' He said, 'The one in the first car.'

Seamus Flynn

Memorial services are the cocktail parties of the geriatric set.

John Gielgud

The trouble with quotes about death is that 99.99 per cent of them are made by people who are still alive.

Joshua Burns

Excuse My Dust
Epitaph

Didn't wake up this morning.

Epitaph for a blues singer

Did you hear about my operation?

Warner Baxter

I told you I was sick.

Spike Milligan

Let's do lunch next week.

Raoul Lionel Felder

Stiff at last.

Anon

By and by, God caught his eye.

George S. Kaufman, epitaph for a waiter

Surrounded by fucking idiots.

Lindsay Anderson

Afterlife and Immortality

Death is not the end. There remains the litigation over the estate.

Ambrose Bierce

I owe much; I have nothing; the rest I leave to the poor.

François Rabelais

Almost everyone when age, disease or sorrows strike him, inclines to think there is a God, or something very like Him.

Arthur Hugh Clough

I do benefits for all religions. I'd hate to blow the hereafter on a technicality.

Bob Hope

Life after death is as improbable as sex after marriage.

Madeleine Kahn, Clue

When I approach the pearly gates, I'd like to hear a champagne cork popping, an orchestra tuning up, and the sound of my mother laughing.

Patricia Routledge

Billy Graham described heaven as a family reunion that never ends. What could hell possibly be like? Home videos of the same reunion?

Dennis Miller

After your death you will be what you were before your birth.

Arthur Schopenhauer

I intend to live forever. So far, so good.

Steven Wright

Millions long for immortality who do not know what to do with themselves on a rainy Sunday afternoon.

Susan Ertz

If we were promised eternal life we would shriek for the promise of death.

A.A. Gardiner

If I have any beliefs about immortality, it is that certain dogs I have known will go to heaven, and very, very few persons.

James Thurber

Ah, well, there is just this world and then the next, and then all our troubles will be over with.

Margot Asquith

I don't believe in an afterlife, although I am bringing a change of underwear.

Woody Allen

Wisdom and Advice

– Old Timer, I have journeyed far to seek the benefit of your immense knowledge and wisdom acquired over a long lifetime. Do you have any words to share?
– Nope.

Richie Ryan and Methos, Highlander

Wisdom doesn't always show up with age. Sometimes age shows up all by itself.

Tom Wilson

When I was young, I was told: 'You'll see, when you're 50.' I'm 50 and I haven't seen a thing.

Erik Satie

I was telling my son about the advantages of being over 50. 'As you get older,' I explained, 'you get wiser.' He just looked at me and said, 'In that case you must be a genius.'

Angus Walker

I gave my beauty and my youth to men. I am going to give my wisdom and experience to animals.

Brigitte Bardot

To my extreme mortification, I grow wiser every day.

Lady Mary Wortley Montagu

By the time you're 80 years old you've learned everything. You only have to remember it.

George Burns

Think, man, think … what would Thora Hird do?

Brian Potter, Phoenix Nights

Whenever I'm confused, I just check my underwear. It holds the answer to all the important questions.

Grampa Simpson, The Simpsons

I have studied many philosophers and many cats. The wisdom of cats is infinitely superior.

Hippolyte Taine

Since I got to 80, I've started reading the Bible a lot more. It's kind of like cramming for my finals.

Vincent Watson

The whiter my hair becomes, the more ready people are to believe what I say.

Bertrand Russell

Grandfather is the wisest person in the house but few of the household listen.

Chinese proverb

Ask the opinion of an older one and a younger than thyself, and return to thine own opinion.

Egyptian proverb

Trust one who has gone through it.

Virgil

I've been things and seen places.

Mae West

I wish I didn't know now what I didn't know then.

Bob Seger

Sometimes one likes foolish people for their folly, better than wise people for their wisdom.

Elizabeth Gaskell

When you win, you're an old pro. When you lose, you're an old man.

Charley Conerly

As we grow older, we grow both more foolish and wiser at the same time.

La Rochefoucauld

In the depth of winter, I finally learned that within me there lay an invincible summer.

Albert Camus

The older you are the more slowly you read a contract.

Leonard Louis Levenson

I am an old man and have known a great many troubles, but most of them never happened.

Mark Twain

As I grow older, I have learned to read the papers calmly and not to hate the fools I read about.

Edmund Wilson

As I grow older, I pay less attention to what men say. I just watch what they do.

Andrew Carnegie

It's worth asking: What do you want? It gets harder and harder to answer as you get older. The answer gets subtler and subtler.

John Jerome

I have a simple philosophy: Fill what's empty. Empty what's full. And scratch where it itches.

Alice Roosevelt

One thing I've learned as I get older is to just go ahead and do it. It's much easier to apologize after something's been done than to get permission ahead of time.

Grace Murray Hopper

I seem to have been only like a boy playing on the sea shore, and diverting myself in now and then finding a smoother pebble or a prettier shell than ordinary, whilst the great ocean of truth lay all undiscovered before me.

Isaac Newton

What a wonderful life I've had! How I wish I had realized it sooner.

Colette

Mottoes to Live By

If you wake up in the morning then you're ahead for the day.

Mace Neufield

You can't turn back the clock. But you can wind it up again.

Bonnie Prudden

You're never too old to become younger.

Mae West

It's never too late to be what you might have been.

George Eliot

I think, therefore I still am.

Elliott Priest

If you rest, you rust.

Helen Hayes

You're only old once!

Dr Seuss

Live well, learn plenty, laugh often, love much.

Ralph Waldo Emerson

If not now, when?
Hillel the Elder
Learning and sex until rigor mortis!
Maggie Kuhn
To stop the ageing – keep on raging.
Malcolm Forbes
Never pass a bathroom.
Duke of Edinburgh
Don't take life so seriously. It's not permanent.
Kathy Holder
May you live all the days of your life.
Jonathan Swift
Live your life and forget your age.

Norman Vincent Peale

May you live to be 100 and may the last voice you hear
be mine.

Frank Sinatra

If you can't make it better, you can laugh at it.
Erma Bombeck

He who laughs, lasts.

Mary Pettibone Poole